ANGELS & ARCHANGELS

ALSO BY DAMIEN ECHOLS

Life After Death

Yours for Eternity (with Lorri Davis)

High Magick

DAMIEN ECHOLS

ANGELS & ARCH-ANGELS

A MAGICIAN'S GUIDE

sounds true
BOULDER, COLORADO

Sounds True
Boulder, CO 80306

Published 2020, 2023

Book design by Karen Polaski and Linsey Dodaro
Cover design by Lisa Kerans

Sigils and photos © 2020, 2023 Damien Echols
Original illustrations © 2020, 2023 Lorri Davis
Author portrait © Lorri Davis
Tarot card illustrations on pages 98–147 by Pamela Colman Smith, 1910
The Shem Ha Mephorash on page 238 © Alamy

Publisher is grateful to acknowledge the cooperation of U.S. Games
Systems, Inc., Stamford, CT 06902 USA, publisher of The Rider-
Waite Tarot Deck®, known also as the Rider Tarot and the Waite Tarot,
Copyright ©1971 by U.S. Games Systems, Inc. The Rider-Waite Tarot
Deck® is a registered trademark of U.S. Games Systems, Inc.

Printed in The United States of America

BK06617

ISBN: 978-1-64963-053-7

The Library of Congress has cataloged the hardcover edition as follows:
Names: Echols, Damien, author.
Title: Angels and archangels : a magician's guide / Damien Echols.
Description: Boulder, CO : Sounds True, 2020. | Includes bibliographical
   references and index.
Identifiers: LCCN 2019034984 (print) | LCCN 2019034985 (ebook) | ISBN
   9781683643265 (hardback) | ISBN 9781683644279 (ebook)
Subjects: LCSH: Angels. | Magic. | Occultism.
Classification: LCC BF1999 .E2434 2020 (print) | LCC BF1999 (ebook) | DDC
   202/.15--dc23
LC record available at https://lccn.loc.gov/2019034984
LC ebook record available at https://lccn.loc.gov/2019034985

10 9 8 7 6 5 4 3 2 1

CONTENTS

ILLUSTRATIONS

FOREWORD BY
JOHN MICHAEL GREER

Like many people, I first heard of Damien Echols in the early 1990s, when he was convicted of a crime he did not commit. I then heard of him at intervals thereafter while the cases of the West Memphis Three lumbered through our nation's overloaded court system. I raised a glass with friends in salute when the news came in 2011 that he had been released, and I was interested by articles in which he credited his magical practices with getting him through his ordeal in prison alive and sane. As far as I knew, the only connection between us was that we were both students and practitioners of ceremonial magic.

Then Damien's book *High Magick* saw print. I fielded an email from a friend who had picked up a copy. "You probably want to see this," the message said, and included a snapshot of the acknowledgments page of the book. That was how I found out that one of my books on ceremonial magic was among the texts Damien had used in his studies while in prison. It's one thing to find out that your work has helped people, and quite another to find it's done that for someone trapped in the living hell of solitary confinement on death row. Of course I sent Damien an email; his response was as gracious as it was prompt. Conversations followed, and one consequence of those was that Damien asked me to write a foreword for his forthcoming book on angel magic, *Angels & Archangels*.

I was delighted to do so, for more reasons than one. During the Middle Ages and Renaissance, angel magic was among the most important branches of Western occultism, practiced and taught by great magicians such as Cornelius Agrippa and John Dee. Today, unhappily, it has become one of the more neglected parts of the tradition. A good practical handbook introducing angel magic to beginning and intermediate students of magic is thus badly needed—and *Angels & Archangels* is that book. Clearly written and informed throughout by Damien's own extensive practical experience, it provides solid guidance to those who are willing to put in the necessary effort.

Angel magic is not a game, nor is it a shortcut or an easy way out. As Damien points out in his introduction, it is a path of doing, as opposed to simply believing. Should you take up the challenge that *Angels & Archangels* offers, expect to work hard, practice daily, and face whatever unfinished business you have in your life. In return, you'll find that the angels open portals to realms of light and wisdom quite literally beyond human comprehension.

ACKNOWLEDGMENTS

Writing a book is by no means a one-person job, and this one couldn't exist without the work of many people. I want to thank a few who put energy into this project in one way or another, starting with my wife, Lorri. She holds our lives together while I immerse myself in research, practice, and writing.

I also want to say thank you to the entire team at Sounds True, especially Tami Simon, Jennifer Yvette Brown, Kriste Peoples, Wendy Gardner, Kira Roark, Brian Galvin, Jade Lascelles, and Jeff Mack. Last but by no means least, my editor Robert Lee, who weaves everything together into a seamless whole.

I'd also like to thank a few people who supported my endeavors following the publication of *High Magick*, including Eddie Vedder, Natalie Maines, and Sturgill Simpson. They made the book tour an adventure I'll remember for the rest of my life.

Thanks also to John Michael Greer, whose work I've learned a tremendous amount from. Finally, I want to express my appreciation and gratitude to all of the readers and reviewers who have been so kind in their feedback and support.

WHAT IS ANGEL MAGICK?

Before I get into the techniques for working with angels and archangels, as well as an extensive catalog of angels and archangels that you'll be working with, I want to discuss some basic information you'll need in order to understand these methods of using magick. My goal is to explain some essential concepts from the get-go so that you won't be distracted or confused later on when you're actually engaging in the practices.

HOW I INVOKED ANGELS TO CREATE MY PREVIOUS BOOK, *HIGH MAGICK*

Let's go back in time a couple of years. By now, you probably know that I was on death row for over eighteen years (the last eight in solitary confinement), the result of which left devastating effects on my psyche—most of it not obvious to me until I was released from prison. I lost a lot of basic abilities that most people take for granted—face and voice recognition, for example (you don't see a lot of faces or hear a lot of voices in solitary—not human ones, at least). So, you could say that going from that type of imprisonment to the streets of Manhattan overnight was a bit of an adjustment. There was no way to prepare for it, and it was psychologically and emotionally crippling. I couldn't function. I had to be taken care of like an invalid. I can barely remember anything about those first couple of years after I got out.

When I was on death row, I had worked my way up to doing magick as much as eight hours a day. When I was released, I couldn't even do it for eight minutes. I couldn't read or write, even though I had been doing both constantly inside. My nervous system had been overloaded and my brain just short-circuited in the process.

So, when Tami Simon, the founder of Sounds True, asked me to write a book on magick, I was ecstatic, but I had no idea how I'd do it. I believed my writing days were sadly behind me. But then she proposed to bring me into the studio and just talk about what I'd practiced and learned while I was on death row—they'd record everything, make transcripts, and we'd use those transcripts to write the book. So, that's what we did—I went to Colorado and spent a week in the studio.

Thing is, because I couldn't write, that meant I couldn't go in with any notes. I couldn't even put together a plan about what I was going to say. I was a blank. Even though I wanted to do the project more than anything, I was terrified—it was like watching an inevitable car crash happen in slow motion. So, I did what most people who are about to be in a collision do—I prayed.

Every morning before I went into the studio, I prayed with my entire being—something like the magickal equivalent of a prayer of desperation. I began invoking angels, one after the other, and put particular attention toward Archangel Raphael, as well as the angels of Mercury—the planetary energy associated with eloquence and successfully conveying ideas to others. It felt like the best choice—magick traditionally falls under Mercury's domain.

So, after invoking these intelligences, I walked into the studio with no plans and just opened my mouth and watched it all come out of me. Like a dam breaking wide open, nearly twenty years of study and practice burst forth. Before I knew it, the week had passed and we had recorded pretty much all of the material you'll find in my book *High Magick*. It's just one of the many miracles that magick has brought about in my life. The book being spoken into being was a miracle, but so was the process, which was restorative and healing.

When I returned home, I could do magick again with the same enthusiasm and focus I'd had on death row. I started with a half hour a day, worked my way up to an hour, then two, three—however long I wanted. And I could write again. Working with angelic energies in my time of need had returned my passions to me and repaired something fundamental in me that made it feel as if I were reborn, at long last, into the world.

NOT JUST ANOTHER RELIGION

People who say they don't believe in magick are simply saying that they haven't practiced magick. Magick doesn't function on belief—it's not a religion; it's a system of practices that work whether you believe in them or not. Paraphrasing a friend of mine, this is exactly why we don't teach more advanced techniques to novices—they work no matter if you're a psychopath or a saint. When you start practicing magick, it's natural to wonder if it's working or if you're just playing mind games with yourself. I know I did. Everything I read just sounded too good to be true—I mean, if it were actually possible to send angels out into the world to fulfill your requests, wouldn't everybody be doing it? Before I passed through the initial stages of practice and began to awaken my energy centers, it just sort of felt as if I was going through the motions of invoking angels. But then I experienced something with me in my cell—an angel, in fact—and I finally knew that magick was real and that it worked. All it took to get to that point was sustained willpower and determination—not an ounce of belief was necessary to the process.

HOW THIS BOOK RELATES TO *HIGH MAGICK*

In *High Magick*, I present the basics of magick as I learned and practiced it in prison. That book is an introduction to this one, and although I'll be repeating a lot of the material here, the advanced content you'll find in this book represents the next step, and it's a steep step that requires successfully climbing the first one. That isn't to say that you can't get a lot out of this book as a stand-alone guide; it's more to steer you in the direction of a more thorough outline on which these practices and rituals are based. So, if you're puzzled or confused about something, it's probably a good idea to use *High Magick* as a primer to this book.

Almost everything you'll find here is based on the Lesser Banishing Ritual of the Pentagram (LBRP) as I presented it in *High Magick*. If you really want to get the most out of magick, you have to be thoroughly familiar with the LBRP. Then you can begin invoking angels and archangels, build upon that practice, and set the greater processes of magick in motion. So, again, it's like lifting weights—a metaphor I repeat all the time. You can't just walk into the gym and start bench-pressing five hundred pounds—you've got to build up to it.

The Hermetic Order of the Golden Dawn, an order of magicians in the 1800s who had a profound impact upon magickal traditions throughout the world, called the LBRP the *Philosopher's Stone*. That's what it is—the key to everything. Build on that practice and anything is possible.

WHY ANGEL MAGICK? MATERIAL MANIFESTATION AND ENLIGHTENMENT

In the traditional literature pertaining to progression along the path of magick, you'll find that someone in the middle stages is said to have obtained "a general mastery of practical magick, though without comprehension."[1] It took me the longest time to understand what that meant.

We perform practical magick to help us in our day-to-day lives, manifesting what we want and need in the physical realm—more money, a better job, the ability to speak eloquently . . . you name it.

Being able to do this efficiently but "without comprehension" points to the deeper reason for doing magick in the first place. As I stress all the time, there's nothing wrong with practices aimed at material manifestation—my surviving death row is living proof of that. The problem comes when we think that this is what magick is all about in its entirety. In fact, material manifestation is more of a side effect than anything else. It's never the primary goal of magick.

The more you advance in the practice of magick, the more you see that it's actually all about transcending our enslavement to the ego and ultimately freeing ourselves from the endless cycles of incarnation. With that in mind, at some point, material manifestations become increasingly undesirable, mostly because they involve losing energy that could be better spent elsewhere.

So, to be clear, there are two reasons we invoke angels and archangels—material manifestation and spiritual sustenance. The difference between these two is fairly straightforward. When practicing manifestation, we invoke energy into our ritual space and then direct it toward something else—for example, a talisman. Doing so, we essentially release the energy and allow it to fulfill its function on the material plane. When we invoke for spiritual sustenance, we absorb all of that energy into our own energy body, and this is what empowers us to transcend our ego and become enlightened. An added benefit of gaining spiritual sustenance is that it also has profound effects on our experience of the physical realm: we feel lighter, happier, and more content; we also care a lot less about things that don't ultimately matter (social media, relational drama, etc.).

By invoking fresh energy into ourselves on a consistent basis, we eventually flush out the old, stagnant energy. When you hear magicians speaking about purification rituals, this is mostly what they're referring to. If we truly dedicate ourselves to this practice on a consistent, prolonged basis, we begin to cleanse the deepest part of our energetic anatomy—the part I'm calling the ego. By pouring enough energy in, the stagnant debris (ego) through which we have tried to see the world since the day we were born begins to disintegrate like a rock under the current of a clear river. The more the ego disintegrates, the more we realize that all we thought we were—that all of this is—was never more than just an illusion.

THE AURA AND ENERGY BODY

Most people picture the aura as an egg-shaped sphere surrounding the body. In reality, this is a rare thing to witness. Unless someone regularly engages in energy work (anything from chi-gung to ceremonial magick), their aura looks more like heat rising off the asphalt in the distance on a hot summer day. A vital part of ceremonial magick is about training and crystallizing the energy system so that it permanently retains the egg-shaped outer layer. If we do this consistently, our energy is held in, and it no longer escapes like vapor. The way we begin this crystallization process is by banishing and invoking, which both involve archangels and angels.

To that point, some magicians argue that we should never do magick for manifestation purposes, that doing so just stands in our way of the ultimate goal. Well, if you've ever been poor, you know that there's actually not much that's helpful or holy about living in a constant state of need, whether it be hunger, lack of protection from the elements, or physical danger of some sort. Furthermore, if you're in some kind of trouble in the physical realm, you probably need to take care of that first before you focus on transcending your egoic chains, if for no other reason than not doing so won't bring you any closer to enlightenment. So, to reiterate, there's absolutely nothing wrong with performing magick to meet your material, real-world needs, and I wouldn't be alive today if there were.

That being said, I recommend striving for a balance between the two approaches, focusing a bit more on spiritual sustenance. Personally, I use what I call the 90/10 rule—90 percent of my magick is for spiritual sustenance, 10 percent is for manifestation. Other magicians take different approaches—for example, one of my friends focuses on practical magick one day out of the week and for all of the other days does magick for spiritual sustenance. As I stress several times in *High Magick*, the important thing is to find out what works best for you.

CONSCIOUS EVOLUTION

Magick is the art and practice of conscious evolution. If the source that spawned human consciousness (what some call God) is like an apple tree, we are the fruit of that tree. Most of the apples fall to the ground, decompose into the soil, and provide energy that further sustains the tree. But some apples take root and become trees themselves. This is the purpose of working with angels and archangels—to stimulate and foster this type of evolution. And this is what empowers us to help other people do the same.

The ultimate goal of working with angels, however, is to become one ourselves. A friend once told me that that's what people actually are—unconscious angels. As we work with the intelligences we call angels, we gradually align our will with the universal will, moving in greater harmony with the source of all creation and assisting in the spiritual evolution of all humanity.

Throughout history and across cultures, we read stories of people transforming into beings of light. In the book of Enoch, the prophet by the same name ascends to heaven to walk with God, and the prophet Elijah is said to have traveled to heaven in a chariot made of fire. Tibetan Buddhism is full of tales of practitioners attaining the rainbow body, or an indestructible energetic body that allows us to approach the highest levels of divinity; and the path to becoming a bodhisattva—essentially, an archangel—is clearly laid out in that tradition. Becoming enlightened is just another part of the journey—the end goal has always been to help others.

THE WILL

In magick, we use the word *will* in much the same way that Hindus use the word *dharma*—it means, among other things, the specific path we're here to walk. Each person's will is unique to them—custom made by their higher self to maximize their potential for awakening. Situations that bring about enlightenment for one person will have no effect on others, simply due to the particular makeup of their will. Unfortunately, most people have no idea what their will is, which makes it easy to get tripped up by the ego (more on that in the following section) and become increasingly trapped in unnecessary drama and psychic impurities.

The most direct path to discovering your will is to connect with your higher self—something we in magick also call the Holy Guardian Angel (HGA), and I've included practices to help you do just that later on in part 2 of this book. In the meantime, I'll just say that you can get a hint of your will in whatever dreams and desires recur for you. I'm not saying that if you've always wanted to be an actor, that means it's what your HGA has in store for you. It might be, but it could simply mean that exploring the path of acting is what will bring you the experiences you'll need in order to wake up and fulfill your will. You might not become the next Marlon Brando or Meryl Streep, but the people and places you encounter will foster an even better outcome.

Interestingly enough, your will is sometimes the exact opposite of the situation you're born into. In order to truly awaken, those who know wealth must experience lack, just as those who are isolated and alone must learn true companionship and love. I grew up destitute and powerless (as evidenced by my false imprisonment), but those experiences were necessary for me to finally understand my will and sense of personal power. Despite what my ego tried to make of those hardships, magick helped me see that I am never truly powerless, no matter what happens all around me.

THE EGO

When we practice magick, what we're essentially doing is rising on the planes of existence toward a level already embodied by angels and archangels. That's not our experience on the lower end of the spectrum (represented by our existence on earth), where we're typically identified with an extremely limited, small self—the ego. The ego is our primary obstacle to discovering our will, fulfilling it, and awakening to our true nature.

Of course, people in the past didn't call it by that name. Even ancient magicians used different terminology for what we call the ego today, because they lived within a particular cultural frame and lacked the vocabulary of psychology and quantum physics. For the most part, the ego was viewed as an external detrimental force, which is why so much magick in the past was devoted to binding and banishing demons. In fact, the ego is somewhat demonic in that it operates like a symbiotic or parasitic entity that only exists on the lower planes. The ego is the very reason why most people are rarely able to settle their mental or emotional state—the ego feeds on the churning energy of constant drama.

The ego isn't a solid thing but an organism of multiple layers and levels—some incredibly dense, others more ethereal and difficult to detect. The densest levels are hardwired into our physical body and involve things such as hunger, lust, and desire to avoid discomfort and pain. This makes sense—the ego has to keep its host form intact, because it can't survive without it. People who are capable of unbelievable physical hardships haven't necessarily rid themselves of the ego; they've simply overcome their attachments to comfort. Take the monk Thich Quang Duc, who sat quietly in meditation while he burned himself to death in Saigon to protest the persecution of Buddhists by the South Vietnamese government in 1963 (made famous by the Pulitzer Prize–winning photograph by Malcolm Browne). It's not that Duc had necessarily destroyed or eradicated those hardwired layers of the ego, but it is quite clear that he had overcome attachment to them—an incredible feat in and of itself.

Most of us will never be able to attain this type of mastery. The ego is simply too interwoven with our physical form, growing incredibly powerful within a short period of time when we're young. Eventually everything we perceive is filtered through the conditioned lens of the ego, while we—the ego's host—remain oblivious to its spreading influence. A primary goal of magickal practice, therefore, is to transcend the harmful states induced by the ego and eventually achieve a different vantage point from which to view the world. That vantage point is on a higher level than we typically find ourselves. Indeed, it is the vantage point of our higher self.

THE POSSESSED

When I was on death row, there was one particularly abusive prison guard who took great pleasure in inflicting pain on those who had no way of fighting back or defending themselves against torture. This is because he had been transformed so completely by the ego that magicians of older times would say he had become possessed. He lived in a hell of his own making, tortured unceasingly by his ego's need for more energy. When the guard's own misery and pain weren't enough for it, the ego caused him to reach out and generate the same suffering in others so that it could feed on that energy as well.

We can only experience life from one of two vantage points: that of the lower self/ego or that of the higher self/enlightened consciousness. The ego is the all-consuming lens through which nearly all of humanity experiences the world, which explains why most people struggle to experience unconditional, true love. Real love—the kind free of attachment—can only be experienced by the higher self. Since the ego never feels complete or satisfied, it's always searching outside itself to fill the void within, and it does so with material goods and people alike, using constant projection to make its claims believable. *If only I had _____ , I would feel complete.* In part, this explains why sappy love songs have always been popular—we actually believe that we need other people to fill the aching holes in our hearts, never realizing that it's a lie the ego tells itself over and over again.

The ego will always need more. On the other hand, the experience of the higher self is marked by a sense of wholeness and completion. Nothing—and no one—can add to the higher self and make it more than it is, because it resides in a constant state of union with the divine. From that vantage point, real love for others is not only possible but also abundant, unconditional, and never-ending.

Fortunately, it is possible for us to transition from an egoic state of consciousness to an enlightened one. In magick, this fundamental shift in vantage point is known as *crossing the abyss*.

CROSSING THE ABYSS

Life after death involves a lot of work—work that must be done while we are alive here on earth. High magick builds our energetic muscles just as regular exercise builds our physical ones. After the physical body dies (which is referred to as the *first death* in magick), we eventually undergo a second death when the material that makes up our astral body begins to disintegrate. How long this second death takes depends on any number of factors—how healthy we were at the time of death, whether our death was tragic and sudden or occurred after a long illness, and so on—but, as a general rule, the stronger the

> THE WORLD ISN'T ANYTHING LIKE WHAT MOST PEOPLE THINK IT IS.

astral body, the longer it will take to go through the process. After the second death, our energy is purified and digested by the source, then recycled and reused for other purposes.

The various promises of spiritual immortality made by religious teachers across time are what magick is designed to fulfill. However, like I said, enlightenment takes work, which is why magick is a path of *doing* (as opposed to simply *believing*). Ideally, the difference between ceremonial magick and other spiritual paradigms is a distinct lack of dogma and an emphasis on practices that allow one to access divinity firsthand and develop a working understanding of the mechanics of the universe. To this end, the initial work of apprentice magicians centers on energy purification, but in the end, high magick is nothing but a series of techniques designed to promote enlightenment. Learning how to shape one's reality along the way is just one of the perks.

Between the ego-dominated state of consciousness we operate from in our day-to-day lives and the evolved condition known as enlightenment stands a fathomless chasm. This is what we call the *abyss* in magick. We magicians see it as our true destiny to leap across that abyss, but, again, it isn't easy. It can be a slow, messy, and fatal act to jump over the gap, and we can't do so until we release all attachments to this side. The binding chains must be broken, and to complete the leap we must be incredibly light. We see this play out in the Egyptian story of having one's heart weighed by Anubis after death—only a person whose heart was as light as a feather (made so by good deeds) passed the test of Maat and was allowed to enter the afterlife. The thing that makes our hearts most heavy is fear. I'll talk more about dealing with fear later on, but for now I'll just say that it's the primary obstacle to crossing the abyss.

Enlightenment (or awakening) means to emerge from a state of unconsciousness—a state of ignorance. The world isn't anything like what most people think it is, and nearly everything we perceive on this side of the abyss is an illusion—or, more accurately, layers upon layers of illusion. Some of that perception is due to the limitations of our physical senses, but much of it is based on lies and misdirection crafted by people with vested interest in keeping humanity unaware or even unconscious. When we cross the abyss, we see through all of this and look upon reality with the clear sight of our infinite, true nature. It's not an intellectual process. It's not something we can get by reading or thinking about it. We experience enlightenment directly, and only because we have completely refined our consciousness.

As I've mentioned before, enlightenment isn't the end, and cross-ing the abyss doesn't mean that you just disperse into angelic stardust. In fact, awakening doesn't mean that you are somehow *perfected*, as if you were suddenly transported safely beyond the cares of the world around you (see the life stories of Jesus and the Buddha for more). In truth, magicians who have crossed the abyss are still fal-lible and human—they just go about their business with a firsthand experience of what lies behind the curtain of the mundane world. This makes—and this is putting it lightly—a substantial difference. That's not to say that someone who has crossed the abyss doesn't go through notable changes—the differences are sometimes quite dras-tic. People have been known to change genders, move to the other side of the world, and completely sever ties to toxic relationships. It all depends on the person.

Additionally I should note that enlightenment isn't for everyone—at least, not in this life. Although most people who devote themselves to magick will meet with tremendous growth and advancement, not everyone is meant to cross the abyss. Accordingly, most of the tech-niques that enable magicians to thrive in this world are meant for those who are not able to free themselves from the ego in this lifetime, which is also why we have practices that promote good karma. Kind deeds, such as donating to charities and feeding the homeless, are wonderful and necessary, but they shouldn't be mistaken for the path to awakening in and of themselves. Good karma is essential, however, in order to obtain a blessed rebirth in which one is finally capable of crossing the abyss.

One way to conceive of good karma is a lack of psychic residue. The practices I've outlined in *High Magick* and offer in greater detail later on in this book will help you clear out this residue. Basically the less residue you have, the clearer you perceive and the more vibrant your energy becomes. How long this takes varies from person to person, but no matter who you are, the practices in this book will help you progress, transform, and eventually—with enough time and effort—cross the abyss.

We collect the psychic residue I'm talking about over time from the ego-based thoughts, feelings, and all sorts of other impurities generated by ourselves and others. I'm referring to it somewhat metaphorically, but if you could actually see all of this gunk, you would look something like an object that had been lying on the ocean floor for years and years—barnacled, silty, and encrusted with mud. So, daily practice is the equivalent of showering yourself off and keeping yourself clean. Like cleaning your body (or house or car), you don't just do it once and call it good. Only by continually freeing yourself of this residue will you be able to get a clear view of your true nature and that of others. This is also what we do for others by performing magick on their behalf. Needless to say, all of this work comes way before we can cross the abyss, and it's infinitely more efficient when we incorporate the beings I'm calling angels and archangels into our practice.

HISTORY OF MAGICK: A NEW ORDER

After the implosion of the Hermetic Order of the Golden Dawn, Aleister Crowley, one of the highest-ranking members, and his student George Cecil Jones combed through the wreckage to determine what had gone wrong. They became convinced that the reason the order failed was that it relied too much on group work, which ultimately resulted in detrimental clashes among the different egos involved. Their solution was to focus on the student-teacher relationship and remove group work from the curriculum, making it possible for members to work individually to learn meditation and magick without knowing or interacting with one another. Members were expected to work on developing themselves mentally, emotionally, spiritually, and physically in order to be of better assistance to humanity, but they still required assistance to cross the abyss. Human nature would always be too weak to cross it alone—our minds and spirits would always be too feeble. That's why, in order to cross, we invoke angels and archangels.

THE DIFFERENCE BETWEEN
ANGELS AND ARCHANGELS

That brings us to the end of this introduction. Before we get into the lists of angels and archangels that follow, it will be helpful to know how the two are different. Here's a basic rundown: angels are almost pure energy, whereas archangels are the powerful, intelligent forces that direct that energy. For example, when we talk about the raw planetary energy of Jupiter, we're talking about angels; when we talk about the consciousness or intelligence governing that energy, we're talking about archangels. Angels are everywhere—they're the very substance of which the cosmos is made. Archangels are essentially stars, just a couple of steps down from gods. They exist on the level of creation immediately above ours, which makes them relatively easy to contact. They're also incredibly willing to work with us, if asked.

Angels are more like elementals—powerful energies with just enough intelligence to perform as directed. This is why you have to give them specific instructions, because they will typically accomplish a given task in the easiest way possible, and they aren't capable of discerning between human concepts of right and wrong. For this reason, I highly recommend telling them to do their work "in a way that harms none." It's also why magicians use archangels to guide and restrict angels to make sure that whatever magick they're doing with them manifests in beneficial ways.

HISTORY OF MAGICK: SCIENCE, MAGICK, AND ALCHEMY

Today we think of science as a field of study that reaches forward into the future, carrying out experiments and observations in order to discover new knowledge. During the Renaissance, however, science was more concerned with the past, believing that humanity was losing knowledge as it progressed. Practitioners of magick, too, were trying to trace humanity's footprints in order to recover the wisdom and practices that were being buried deeper each year beneath the shifting sands of time. Magicians and scientists alike agreed that the only knowledge worth discovering and preserving was that which enabled us to repair our fallen condition and return us to our original, divine state. Magicians turned inward, looking for salvation by exploring the internal planes, whereas scientists fixed their gaze on the outer world, believing that by understanding the external they could come to a greater understanding of internal mechanisms and reverse the degenerative condition of humanity. The love child of this brief affair between magick and science was alchemy.

LOOKING FORWARD

Part 1 of this book is devoted to introducing you to the angels and archangels I work with on a regular basis. Part 2 makes a deep dive into the various magickal practices and rituals I use to invoke those angels and archangels. Think of part 1 as your dictionary or encyclopedia; part 2 is more like your user's manual. Hopefully this introduction (when paired with *High Magick*) will clear up any misunderstandings or questions you have along the way.

PART I

ANGELS AND ARCHANGELS

The following descriptions of angels and archangels come from my own practice and the personal notes I've collected from various sources that span hundreds of years. Many of the authors are unknown; others will be familiar to anyone already versed in invoking these energies, and you'll find most of these magicians and scholars listed in the resources section at the back of this book. I encourage you to cross-reference the sources and use the ones that best speak to you. A couple of points to keep in mind on the descriptions to follow:

- The **spellings** of the names of these angels and archangels vary from source to source, and they often change over time as authors borrow and learn from magicians who came before them. Often the names were translated from other languages or spelled phonetically, so you'll find a lot of variety depending on which source you're using. In short, there's no correct way to spell these names; the important thing is that you're able to approximate a workable pronunciation from the way it's written.

- Some people can get hung up on the **pronunciations** of these names. Don't let that stress you out. The most important thing about working with these intelligences is your intention. As long as your intention is to connect with the angel or archangel, you're already halfway there. Using your spoken voice in the pursuit of that connection is just one more element to strengthen the process.

- Please also keep in mind that the following **names** aren't actually the names of specific entities in the same sense that humans use names—they're more like titles than anything else. For example, the name Raphael translates into English as something like "the healing of God," so when you say "Raphael," you aren't necessarily calling upon a particular entity named Raphael but rather invoking the healing power inherent in all divinity, calling upon a particular aspect of the *All*. There aren't actually winged creatures up there in the clouds somewhere who are going to get put out if you don't pronounce their names in just the right way.

PRACTICE, EXPERIMENT, AND FIND OUT FOR YOURSELF.

- You'll also see that the angels and archangels are often assigned male or female **genders**. Like the other anthropomorphic details to follow, gender is just another tool to assist your visualization work. The intelligences clearly aren't traditionally *male* or *female*, because energy is essentially neither. That being said, we're enculturated to consider some manifestations of energy as feminine and some as masculine, and I think that the problems that come with that can be acknowledged while still using those associations to our benefit. It's also just shorthand for talking about polarities, as in the Taoist frame of *yin* and *yang*. That being said, feel free to play with the genders as you see fit.

Traditionally, some people say that the archangels Michael and Raphael, for example, are masculine, whereas Gabriel is feminine and Uriel embodies both genders equally. Then you'll find other presentations that assert that all of them are masculine except for Gabriel. I find the latter attributions to be more helpful in my own visualizations, but, as elsewhere, I encourage you to do what works best for you. The point is to do whatever it takes to envision them more clearly and to not get hung up on details that fundamentally have very little to do with these particular manifestations of the divine.

- Finally, you're about to come across all sorts of **physical descriptions** pertaining to these energies. I want to acknowledge that people are often put off by some of this traditional Western/Judeo-Christian imagery (for understandable reasons), as I initially was. I talk about this a lot more in *High Magick*, but here I'll just suggest trying it out and seeing how this imagery works for you. Like the gender issue, these are visual details we've inherited that don't amount to much, and yet they run so deep in our psyches that they often come naturally to us whether we want them to or not. That being said, feel free to envision the angels and archangels in whatever way works best for you. Some people prefer to employ the lamassu iconography—a composite of four beings: a bull, a lion, a man, and an eagle; see the cover of this book for an image of a lamassu—from Mesopotamia that predates the Judeo-Christian descriptions, and that approach more closely approximates what the magicians of that time period would have done (for example, Raphael is a lamassu composed of yellow light, Gabriel is one made of blue light, and so on). Keep in mind that each of these descriptions is just a starting point toward establishing a connection to the energy represented by the image, and it's often the case that a suggested visualization is what opens the door to first registering their presence.

Any of the suggested reasons for invocation you'll find in part 1 should be considered suggestive and by no means set in stone or complete. These correspondences are only hints of possible manifestations, and they often come from my own personal experiences working with these intelligences. I strongly believe that just about any angel or archangel can be invoked for any purpose and that the primary difference arises in the way each manifests their response on the physical plane. For example, just looking at the Tree of Life/planetary energies, if you wanted to invoke them for improved physical health, the energy of Mars might attack and destroy any problematic ailments, whereas the archangel of the sun would boost your vitality and ability to heal yourself, and the intelligences correlated to Saturn would simply work to banish any further detrimental factors to your physical health.

The main point to this introduction is to urge you to take these descriptions and correspondences lightly. View part 1 as a primer or helpful guide, not as rigid scripture. As you progress in your own training and practice, I hope you'll add what comes from your own experiences to these lists, and, as always, I encourage you to practice, experiment, and find out for yourself.

CHAPTER 1

ARCHANGELS OF
THE ELEMENTS

If you've read *High Magick* or practiced other versions of ceremonial magick, you're probably already familiar with this set of archangels—almost every version of the Lesser Banishing Ritual of the Pentagram (LBRP) I've come across includes them. Here's a little more detail than I gave in *High Magick*, and you can certainly use the information found in that book to support the practices you'll find in part 2 of this one. I'm calling them the "Archangels of the Elements" here primarily to distinguish them from energies with the same titles you'll find later on (namely, in the Tree of Life set).

The primary reason that we begin by working with this set of archangels is that they are the ones closest to us—or, rather, closest to the level of the material world in which we exist. That was the traditional explanation given to students of magick in the past couple of centuries, but I think that nowadays it's also helpful to think of them as representing different energies corresponding to aspects of the lower parts of our soul. By invoking them we learn to balance ourselves on the most fundamental level, and anyone who spends just a few weeks doing so will notice positive changes in their lives:

- A lesser tendency to control your
surroundings or other people

- More faith and self-confidence

- A greater sense of well-being and peace

- Various other benefits that come from living in
  the present moment (discussed in chapter 5)

You'll also find some other uses for invoking the elemental arch-angels below. Then, in part 2 of this book you'll learn other ways of working with these energies, varying in strength and complication, as well as supplemental exercises to strengthen your ability to concentrate and invoke. Eventually we'll get to the most effectual ritual in magick I know of—the Shem Operation.

HISTORY OF MAGICK: WITHOUT HIDDEN MOTIVE

When Emperor Constantine gutted the Bible, nearly fifty books were either removed entirely or substantially edited. Much of that material was attributed to Christ himself, most notably instructions given to his students on how to shape reality. For example, we still read "Ask, and it shall be given you" in Matthew 7:7 (NRSV), but what's been removed are the instructions on how to ask. The scientist and religious scholar Gregg Braden says that the original source reads "All things you ask straightly and directly from inside my name you shall be given. So far you have not done this. Ask without hidden motive and be surrounded by your answer. Be enveloped by what you desire, that your gladness be full." Furthermore, Braden asserts that "without hidden motive" is better translated as "without judgment"—not labeling things with the egoic labels of good and bad.[1] In other words, when we ask, we should do so from the perspective of the higher self if we want to manifest something within the divine matrix. Therefore we must use the language of the matrix, which is consciousness translated through the electromagnetic fields generated by our heart and mind. In short, the language of the quantum field is energy itself. Christ taught that one should act as if what has been requested has already been granted. By doing so, the electromagnetic field of the heart sends a signal to the quantum field, which will then manifest the prayer on the physical plane. We do the same thing with our mind by visualizing what we want to manifest—the brain's electromagnetic field then sends that signal to the divine matrix.

The Sigil of Archangel Raphael

RAPHAEL

Raphael, whose name means "the healing of God," is the archangel of air. Raphael is also associated with the East and the season of spring. Because air energy is connected with the power of the intellect, Raphael is also the archangel of logic and reason. Some books left out of the Bible present Raphael walking back roads and meeting with strangers. In one story, a traveler runs into Raphael and tells the archangel that he's in love with a woman, but every time someone attempts to marry her, a demon interferes and kills the suitor. He asks Raphael for help, and Raphael gives him the recipe for a special incense to make—if the man burns it near the woman, the demon will flee. It works, and the man and woman are finally able to get married.

Keys to Visualizing Raphael

- Radiant yellow robes
- Holds a caduceus (a staff with two entwined snakes)
- Anything associated with spring (for example, a damp, warm wind)

Some Reasons to Invoke Raphael

- To better articulate your ideas to others
- For safe passage
- For healing of any sort
- For assistance with meditation and mental clarity (for example, to help ace an exam)
- To enhance the intellect and learn the deeper truths of philosophical and spiritual teachings

The Sigil of Archangel Gabriel

GABRIEL

Gabriel is the archangel of water and the West. She is most associated with autumn, love, and our subconscious mind. Her domain is the most occluded part of our psyche, where intuition, emotions, and dreams come from. In the biblical story of the annunciation, it's Gabriel who tells Mary that she will give birth to the Christ. For this reason, Gabriel always comes to mind in the late fall as Christmas approaches, because when I was on death row I used to eagerly count down to Christmas, focusing on pleasant childhood memories (my grandmother's homemade sugar cookies, for example) instead of the garbage I was eating. When I could visualize those memories clearly enough, it worked kind of like a life preserver, and for a while I could forget about the people who were trying to kill me. In this way, Gabriel helped keep me sane when I was in hell.

Keys to Visualizing Gabriel
- Blue robes
- Holds a chalice
- Anything associated with autumn (cool air, the smell of fallen leaves, etc.)

Some Reasons to Invoke Gabriel
- To overcome anger or melancholy
- To heal any form of emotional wounding
- For anything related to pure love

The Sigil of Archangel Michael

MICHAEL

Many people in the Western world are familiar with Michael, the archangel of fire. Michael represents warrior energy, and he is also associated with the summer and the southern direction. Anything pertaining to courage, willpower, ambition, or sex drive is the arena of Michael, who is also one of the easiest archangels to contact. In Catholic churches throughout the world, September 29 is known as Michaelmas, the feast of the archangels, but it's specifically named after Michael.

Keys to Visualizing Michael

- Red robes
- Holds a sword
- Anything associated with summer (heat, dryness, intense light, etc.)

Some Reasons to Invoke Michael

- To lose weight or get into shape
- For ferocity in competition
- For protection
- To enhance passion
- For any outcome associated with fire

The Sigil of Archangel Uriel

URIEL

Uriel has a special place for those of us who practice magick—he watches over and guides us, especially when it comes to divination. Uriel is the archangel of the earth element, and the season connected with him is winter. We associate Uriel with the north, and his arena is anything having to do with the physical realm, particularly health and finances.

Keys to Visualizing Uriel

- Forest-green robes
- Holds a pentacle (a five-pointed star on a round disk)
- Anything associated with winter (cold, crisp air; a frozen landscape; clear sky, etc.)

Some Reasons to Invoke Uriel

- To assist with divination
- For anything involving finances
- To obtain material goods and wealth

The Sigil of Archangel Metatron

METATRON

Metatron is the only archangel in all the stories of angels to have ever been human. He is sometimes said to have been the prophet Enoch, who penned the Gnostic gospel known as the book of Enoch. In certain traditions it is said that the divine source of creation rewarded Enoch for his faith by never having to die a physical death—instead, Enoch was transformed into the archangel who is closest to the very throne of heaven. Whether this is true or not, Metatron is the name magicians have used to call upon the intelligence who directs the flow of the purest, most formless energy down into the denser levels of reality.

He is associated with no element and no direction, since he exists within the mind of divinity itself. As the kingdom of God is actually both within and all around us, there is no place where it is not—hence, Metatron is everywhere. However, since we generally equate the heavenly realms with an upward direction, I have always attributed that direction to him in my enhanced version of the LBRP. Most people who employ this modification generally feel that Metatron just feels right when visualized above.

Since Metatron directs the flow of divine energy that we're ultimately striving toward in the form of enlightenment, he is the perfect intelligence to connect with and absorb the energy of. We become more like him with each invocation, because it raises our own energetic vibration to a matching frequency. This effect only lasts a short while, so if this appeals to you, repeat the process often.

Keys to Visualizing Metatron
- Blinding white, crystalline robes
- Stands or sits on a throne made of light

Some Reasons to Invoke Metatron
- To raise the vibrational frequency of a given area (a room, house, neighborhood, etc.)
- To initiate the process of crossing the abyss
- To complete the Great Work, that is, to escape the wheel of samsara (aimless wandering)

The Sigil of Archangel Sandalphon

SANDALPHON

Sandalphon is the archangel who regulates energy flow from divinity to the physical realm. Nothing passes from heaven to earth without being noticed by Sandalphon. It's also said that Sandalphon is responsible for gathering prayers and carrying them to the source of creation, as well as being the archangel of music. Sandalphon is the commander of the group of angels known as the Ashim, which means "souls of fire." Additionally, all types of fertility are under the domain of this powerful being. Some sources identify Sandalphon as the prophet Elijah, who ascended to heaven on a chariot of fire.

Keys to Visualizing Sandalphon

- Pale brown robes
- Holds a cornucopia (an overflowing basket of food)

Some Reasons to Invoke Sandalphon

- To strengthen your powers of manifestation
- To prevent financial or material loss
- For greater strength and endurance, especially during adverse times
- For assistance in creating music or to improve your musical ability
- To obtain a home
- For assistance in working with plants
- To spread a particular message in the world

CHAPTER 2

ARCHANGELS OF THE TREE OF LIFE

The archetypal Tree of Life presented here in its Qabalistic form has been around since Assyria in the ninth century BCE. In ceremonial magick, one way to view the Tree of Life is as a metaphor for the human nervous system that corresponds with three levels of existence: the branches that reach into the heavens are the brain's neural pathways, the roots in the underworld correlate to the nerves emanating from the spinal column, and the worldly trunk is the spine itself (one reason why various forms of meditation encourage you to keep your back straight). The alchemical texts of old also use the symbol of the tree in similar fashion. In short, the metaphor is a pedagogical device employed to help us awaken and refine the energies that reside in the various parts of our nervous system. Linking and connecting these empowers us to annihilate the illusions of the ego and awaken to our true nature.

Some version of the Tree of Life plays a major role in most of the world's spiritual traditions. The Buddha attained his enlightenment under the Bodhi tree, the Druids considered trees extremely sacred (in fact, the word *Druid* means "one who holds the knowledge of the trees"), and the Norse god Odin hung upon Yggdrasil—the tree at the center of the Norse cosmos that connects its nine worlds—for nine days to discover the secret of the runes. In particular, Odin's story emphasizes just how important sacrifice is if we truly want to acquire transcendent wisdom—we have to be willing to completely let go of our sense of self.

Working with the archangels of the Tree of Life has been some of my favorite magick for years now. When it comes to manifesting, nothing has come close to the success rate I have when invoking these energies. They quickly carry out any tasks given to them, and working with them brings me a tremendous amount of joy and wonder. Once I began invoking them on a daily basis, I felt happier, more confident, and more emotionally secure than ever. In particular, my self-criticizing thoughts became fainter and less frequent. Additionally, I experienced fear less often and generally just felt that everything was going to be okay. After I got out of prison, it was working with the archangels of the Tree of Life that began my long process of healing myself from post-traumatic stress disorder (PTSD).

Unlike the archangels of the elements, who resemble general practitioners, these archangels are more like specialists in their given fields. When you really want to narrow the focus of your magick, these are the energies to invoke, and we'll go over how to do so later in part 2.

One thing you'll probably notice right away is that some of these archangels share names with the elemental archangels (for example, Raphael of Tiphareth and Michael of Hod), and sometimes my suggested visualizations have them appearing quite differently. The reason for this is simple: They're not the same archangels. We might call them by the same name (i.e., title), but only in the way that many unrelated people can share the same first or last names.

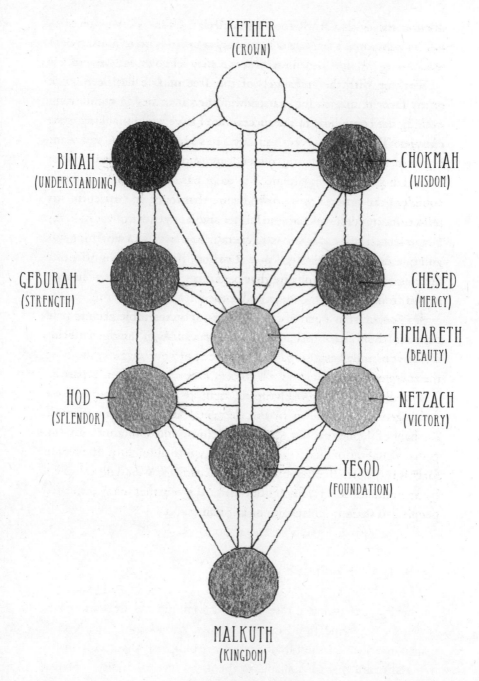

KETHER
(CROWN)

BINAH
(UNDERSTANDING)

CHOKMAH
(WISDOM)

GEBURAH
(STRENGTH)

CHESED
(MERCY)

TIPHARETH
(BEAUTY)

HOD
(SPLENDOR)

NETZACH
(VICTORY)

YESOD
(FOUNDATION)

MALKUTH
(KINGDOM)

The Qabalic Tree of Life

SANDALPHON, ARCHANGEL OF MALKUTH

On the Tree of Life, the densest level of reality is known as Malkuth. It's where things such as our bodies exist. Pretty much anything you can touch with your physical hand is within the sphere of Malkuth, where Archangel Sandalphon presides. Sandalphon is traditionally thought of as being Metatron's twin, because the two work together as a team. Metatron sends the flow of divine energy down from Kether into Malkuth, and then Sandalphon directs that flow into all the different aspects of the material world, making certain that each aspect doesn't receive too much or too little. In some Judaic systems of magick, it's taught that another world existed before the one we currently inhabit, and that due to its imperfection it could not hold the flow of divinity directed into it, so it shattered like a broken pot. The shards left over from the previous world lie on a level of reality below ours on the energetic spectrum, and our world is built upon those pieces of the old one. Sandalphon was assigned the task of making sure the shattering wouldn't happen again.

Keys to Visualizing Sandalphon of Malkuth

- Pale brown robes
- Holds a cornucopia

Some Reasons to Invoke Sandalphon of Malkuth

- To manifest anything in the material world
- To bless your practical magick such that it manifests in a way that harms none

GABRIEL, ARCHANGEL OF YESOD

The next sphere, situated directly above Malkuth on the Tree of Life, is Yesod. The name Yesod means roughly "foundation," the level of reality upon which the physical world is built. All that exists in the material realm first took shape on the astral level of reality, which is what Yesod is.

The intelligence that manifests the strongest at this level is Archangel Gabriel. Although different from the Gabriel of the elemental set of archangels, there are several similarities—for example, this Gabriel also rules the realm of our intuition and psychic perception. Gabriel is also the archangel of the moon, and much as the moon exerts a pull on the tides in the physical world, it also exerts an influence on the ebb and flow of etheric energy within the astral plane. For this reason, magick for prosperity and growth is traditionally done when the moon is full, because that's when the tide of etheric energy is at its peak.

Keys to Visualizing Gabriel of Yesod

- Purple robes
- Wears a silver headband with a crescent moon on it

Some Reasons to Invoke Gabriel of Yesod

- To increase the presence of love in your life
- To bring peace and subdue aggression
- To enhance artistic inspiration
- To find answers in dreams and help interpret dreams
- To strengthen your magick
- To obtain secret information
- To gain insight on the workings of the astral realm
- For emotional strength in times of crisis

MICHAEL, ARCHANGEL OF HOD

As we ascend the tree from Yesod, the next sphere we arrive at is Hod, the realm of the intellect, logic, and reasoning. It's also the realm of travel, business ventures, medicine, science, and magick. In fact, Hod is associated with all the gods of magick (Hermes, Mercury, Thoth, etc.). The archangel of Hod is Michael, although he takes on a somewhat different manifestation than the archangel of the element of fire, having more to do here with mediation and facilitation than with protection.

Keys to Visualizing Michael of Hod

- Orange robes
- Holds a caduceus (a staff with two entwined snakes)

Some Reasons to Invoke Michael of Hod

- To make intelligent decisions, especially during stressful times
- For protection when performing magick (as well as to strengthen your magick)
- To recover from illness
- For new business ideas and to meet with success in any business venture
- To make good financial deals (say, when buying a house or car)
- To eloquently express yourself and your ideas

HANIEL, ARCHANGEL OF NETZACH

The sphere directly above Yesod on the Tree of Life is my personal favorite to work with. Netzach is the level of reality on which our emotional life plays out, but it's also the sphere of art, beauty, sensuality, and luxury. It also represents the plane of existence where the *fey* (what we have come to think of as faeries) exist. Much like angels and archangels, the fey have been anthropomorphized and reduced to tiny people with gossamer wings (think of Tinker Bell). In reality, faeries are incredibly powerful entities, some benevolent toward humanity and others whose sense of right and wrong are so different from ours that they can sometimes come across as malicious.

The archangel who presides over this level of reality is Haniel. Haniel possesses characteristics and energy that are equally masculine and feminine, so you will see this entity referred to by various pronouns in magickal texts. (Haniel responds to any of them, so feel free to use whichever feels right to you.)

Keys to Visualizing Haniel of Netzach
- Seafoam-green robes
- Accompanied with the scent of rose

Some Reasons to Invoke Haniel of Netzach
- To bring peace to arguing lovers
- To encourage fidelity and enhance passion
- To turn rivals and enemies into allies and friends
- To gain new friends
- To reunite loved ones
- For assistance in creating any form of artwork
- To experience joy
- To create an environment in your home
  that is pleasing to all of the senses
- To aid in gardening or any nature-related activities
- To develop a mutually beneficial relationship with the fey

RAPHAEL, ARCHANGEL OF TIPHARETH

From the realm of Netzach, we ascend to the very heart of the Tree of Life. Tiphareth is a brilliant golden sphere that shines like the noonday sun (in fact, the planetary energy of the sun is correlated with the sphere of Tiphareth). The energies of all the other spheres on the Tree of Life pass through Tiphareth, which regulates and harmonizes them all. When we do magick utilizing the golden sphere in our chest (for example, in the Qabalistic Cross), we are using the energy center that corresponds to Tiphareth, the great balancer of all energies. Tiphareth represents the highest, most evolved state of consciousness that people are capable of achieving—what some traditions call Christ-consciousness. When we awaken the flow of Tiphareth's energy within us, we begin working deliberately toward the evolution of our consciousness, and we gradually grow to see the beauty that exists in all things. This level of reality touches and connects us to all others.

The archangel who presides over this sphere is Raphael. Because Raphael is associated with healing, we pull the energies of all the spheres on the Tree of Life through Tiphareth to send healing energy to others or receive it ourselves. Raphael is also correlated with victory, success, and prosperity.

Keys to Visualizing Raphael of Tiphareth

- Golden robes and brilliant armor with the image of the sun on the breastplate
- Holds a scepter

Some Reasons to Invoke Raphael of Tiphareth

- For all manner of healing—physical, mental, emotional, and spiritual
- To repair rifts between yourself and others
- To complete projects
- To attain fame or popularity through talent
- To win legal battles
- For stability of any sort
- To pacify aggressive situations and gain victory over enemies
- To improve physical vitality and stamina
- For any sort of material prosperity
- To overcome sorrow

KAMAEL, ARCHANGEL OF GEBURAH

As we continue to ascend the tree, we move from Tiphareth to the sphere of Geburah. Geburah is the sphere of strength and severity. Its energy is a deep, rich red. Working with this energy brings courage, self-discipline, protection, willpower, and the strength to cut away that which does not serve our growth and development. If this energy is not in balance, it leads to cruelty, lack of compassion, and anger.

The archangel of this sphere is Kamael. His name translates roughly as "strength of God," and he is the fiercest warrior among the celestial hosts. Kamael exists to protect those who may not be able to protect themselves, and when called upon he will defend you against anything or anyone who attempts to inject strife into your life. Kamael works swiftly and without remorse to keep us safe and shielded, but he can only do so with our invitation.

In certain magickal circles, it's rumored that Kamael wasn't the first archangel to rule the domain of Geburah. Some say the original power of this sphere was the angel Samael, but that he "fell," and this fall led to Kamael's rise. What exactly is a "fallen" angel? Think of it like this—angels have neither free will nor self-awareness. They're kind of like computer programs designed to carry out specific functions around the universe. Some speculate that the story of fallen angels is about a misstep in the evolutionary process that led to a small group of these angelic intelligences becoming self-aware (somewhat like Adam and Eve in the book of Genesis), and this self-awareness led to a false sense of separation from divinity.

Keys to Visualizing Kamael of Geburah

- Red robes, crimson armor, and a helmet
- Holds a spear and shield

Some Reasons to Invoke Kamael of Geburah

- To repel negative energy
- To defeat enemies and defend against bullies
- For bravery in the face of adversity
- As a shield against aggressive people and situations
- To project an aura of power
- To express anger in a healthy way
- To repel thieves and protect your home
- For assistance in any type of competition
- For protection against negative thoughts

TZADKIEL, ARCHANGEL OF CHESED

Chesed is where we find the energies of abundance and prosperity, joy and adventure. It's reminiscent of the planetary energy of Jupiter, which falls under its domain. When we truly tap into this sphere, we learn how to love unconditionally and throw ourselves ferociously and fearlessly into the fray of life.

When working with Tzadkiel, the archangel of this sphere, burning bayberry and cedar incenses will strengthen the experience. Keep an eye out for an increase in favorable events and circumstances—Tzadkiel is the archangel of luck. The more you work with him, the luckier you'll become. It's said in magickal circles that it was Tzadkiel who kept watch over Abraham, the father of Judaism, Christianity, and Islam. There comes a time when everyone who walks the path of magick must decide to do so with complete devotion in order to make further progress, and it's Tzadkiel who helps us choose the spiritual or magickal realm over the physical world. That being said, I still think of Tzadkiel as the fun archangel.

Keys to Visualizing Tzadkiel of Chesed

- Blue robes
- Holds a scepter, like a king

Some Reasons to Invoke Tzadkiel of Chesed

- For any form of prosperity and abundance
- To attain inner harmony and joy
- For luck in gambling
- To enhance your popularity and the esteem of others
- For the power to help others
- To increase any talent or skill
- To better understand your will and purpose in life
- For more ambition
- To make certain that others keep their promises

TZAPHKIEL, ARCHANGEL OF BINAH

Binah is the most feminine of all the spheres, and it's here that we find all the dark goddesses, such as Hecate and Nyx. Binah is affiliated with the energy of Saturn, which is also associated with things such as binding and banishing, time, karma, and old age. The principal work of Binah is the complete dissolution of the ego, and it's Binah that is most closely related to the process of crossing the abyss. It's here where the ego and its programming become transparent and we can finally see the self for the illusion it has always been.

Tzaphkiel is the archangel of Binah. She helps us understand the painful lessons that are a necessary component to any measure of spiritual development. Working with Tzaphkiel teaches us the value of silence, because we must first learn to be silent in order to properly hear. Hers is not an energy to invoke lightly. For example, I invoked Tzaphkiel to bind the attorney general who was trying to have me executed (even though the evidence showed that I was innocent), and he was eventually caught in a scandal that destroyed his career and personal life. Tzaphkiel is also the first angel I ever saw after a couple months of working with these angelic intelligences, and my first glimpse of her was like a revelation—any doubts I had about magick before that moment vanished. The experience was actually terrifying. I've never been able to fully articulate the event, because our language is mostly designed to address and describe mundane occurrences, thoughts, and feelings. Whatever it was, experiencing Tzaphkiel in my cell on death row was certainly not mundane.

Keys to Visualizing Tzaphkiel of Binah
- Black robes
- Holds an hourglass

Some Reasons to Invoke Tzaphkiel of Binah
- To bind enemies in order to prevent them from doing harm
- To destroy the plans and schemes of enemies
- To repel curses or other forms of negative energy
- To bring justice upon those who have done you wrong
- To banish sickness and anxiety
- To project an aura of authority and gain the respect of others
- For a restful night's sleep
- To discover secrets

RAZIEL, ARCHANGEL OF CHOKMAH

If Binah is the embodiment of divine feminine energy on the tree, then Chokmah is the divine masculine. It's Chokmah that is most associated with the father gods and deities. Chokmah is also the energy behind the magician card in the tarot—the energy that reaches out into the universe to put things in motion. However, keep in mind that in Chokmah, there is no more *you*, which is why it was from here that Christ said, "I and my father are one" (John 10:30, KJV). The place where the illusion of the ego once existed becomes completely filled by the divine, and it's in Chokmah where the distinction between creator and creation dissolves.

The archangel that presides over everything within the realm of Chokmah is Raziel, the prince of hidden things. Raziel is the force that causes us to have epiphanies and realizations about how magick and the universe operate, and this information often comes to us in dreams, signs, and hidden flashes of intuition or inner knowing. Raziel is also said to witness and record everything that takes place on Earth in an infinitely enormous book, and the book will only be closed once the last sentient being enters the realm of the divine. In other words, he's heaven's recordkeeper.

Keys to Visualizing Raziel of Chokmah

- Gray robes
- Holds an extremely large book

Some Reasons to Invoke Raziel of Chokmah

- To set plans in motion and speed up processes
- To gain energy after you have been drained
- To break free of any situation that feels like a rut
- To obtain wisdom and deeper insight about any subject, especially anything pertaining to past civilizations and cultures
- To discover forgotten or unrecorded magickal techniques
- To strengthen any divination technique

METATRON, ARCHANGEL OF KETHER

Kether is the top sphere on the Tree of Life. This sphere represents complete and utter union with the divine source of creation. It is beyond form or duality. It's said that the human mind is incapable of conceiving of Kether because it contains no qualities that the human intellect can grasp. To achieve the state of consciousness symbolized by Kether would be to lose all sense of an individual self and completely merge with divinity. When no trace of self or ego remains, the individual becomes a window or portal through which the divine mind shines into the material realm. In this context, Metatron is the archangel of Kether and is therefore the one who directs the flow of divine energy down into the material plane.

Keys to Visualizing Metatron of Kether

- Robes of crystal clear light
- Sits on a throne made of amazingly brilliant light

Some Reasons to Invoke Metatron of Kether

- To break free from the wheel of samsara, the endless cycle of suffering and rebirth
- To complete the Great Work
- To align your individual will with the universal will
- To see through the illusions of the material world
- To raise the vibrational rate of your consciousness in order to display more aspects of divinity in your life

PLANETARY ENERGIES

Although I'm not going into depth about planetary energies, you'll come across several references to them in this chapter and elsewhere in the book. Think of them as the lower octaves of the pure, divine energy represented by the spheres on the Tree of Life. Pretty much everything about the planetary energies—including the colors attributed to them—are the same as the spheres to which they correspond. In addition, each of the planetary energies has a divine name associated with it that you can use in some of the invoking rituals later on in the book.

- Saturn is associated with the sphere of Binah and the divine name YHVH Elohim
- Jupiter with Chesed and the divine name El
- Mars with Geburah and Elohim Gibor
- The sun with Tiphareth and YHVH Eloah Va Da'ath
- Venus with Netzach and YHVH Tzabaoth
- Mercury with Hod and Elohim Tzabaoth
- The moon with Yesod and Shadai El Chai

I regularly invoke different sets of angels and archangels for the same purpose. For example, if I'm performing a protection ritual, I'll invoke the archangels of Mars, Geburah, and the element of fire (i.e., Michael), because all of these intelligences act in harmony like interlocking pieces of the same puzzle. You'll see how this "angel stacking" plays out in more detail in chapters 7 and 8.

CHAPTER 3

ANGELS AND ARCHANGELS
OF THE ZODIAC

One of the things ceremonial magick is well known for is cataloging correspondences, including which archangel presides over each sign of the zodiac. When dealing with archangels in this particular frame, what we're actually invoking is the energy of certain stars and systems of celestial bodies. Doing so on a regular basis promotes the process known as enlightenment, and it's through invoking these intelligences in a particular ritual I describe in chapter 8 that I first experienced a disintegration of the ego that I still can't put into words (probably because language is inherently dualistic). You'll also find the angels and archangels in this chapter in their associated tarot manifestations in chapter 4.

It may sound like something cheesy you'd find on a greeting card, but it's true: we come from the stars. The light of stars comes from the nuclear fusion taking place at their cores, and it's the same fusion that created most of the elements we find in the known universe. Due to our quantum entanglement with these celestial bodies, we're forever connected to them and capable of drawing energy from them. For the longest time, the techniques for harnessing and applying celestial energy have been passed down from master to student, mostly in an esoteric manner.

For example, whenever animals make an appearance in the Bible, it's actually encoded information about the stars. When Adam first names the creatures in Eden, it's a description of the way the first civilizations named the constellations (ram, bull, fish, etc.) and learned to invoke their energies. The story of Noah saving the animals is really about the preservation of ancient teachings through a particular turbulent time in the known world. Moses traversing the desert with the ark of the covenant is about carrying these teachings forward into the next age (namely, the transition from polytheism to monotheism).

HISTORY OF MAGICK: THE EON OF HORUS

Just as the sun travels through the signs of the zodiac, so too does human consciousness evolve throughout time. Some assert that we are currently in the third eon of recorded history, although there were many other eras prior to the first eon of Isis, in which our primary means of worship was directed toward goddess figures (for example, the Venus of Willendorf, created somewhere between 28000 and 25000 BCE). The eon of Isis hit its peak somewhere around 2500 BCE, giving way to the eon of Osiris, when humanity's focus turned more to masculine representations of divinity (most notably, figures who die and are resurrected, such as Osiris and Jesus Christ). In the past few hundred years, the eon of Osiris has given way to the eon of Horus, an eon marked by a growing interest in spirituality. Whereas the earlier two eons were conceived of in feminine and masculine images, the eon of Horus is represented as a child, sometimes as twins—the twins of science and magick. The arrival of a new eon doesn't invalidate previous magickal practices (for example, even now, the magick of the eons of Isis and Osiris can be used to great success); it's just that the present formula of magick will be better suited to the psyches of current generations.

There is a presence that guides the evolution of humanity, and it leads us toward eventual union with itself, which we can only know through direct experience. Like many of you, I have experienced messengers who have pointed me closer and closer to this presence, and most of these messengers are what we know as angels and archangels. Technically, any energy that acts as an intermediary between us and this guiding presence falls into these categories, no matter their appearance. To be clear, they're not all blond, blue-eyed human types that fly around encased in white light. The messenger I have recently learned the most from is a being the ancient Sumerians called Enlil, whose name means "lord of heaven."

Every couple of eons (somewhere between every 2,000 and 2,500 years), humanity is provided a new dispensation—a way of worshipping and interacting with the Prime Mover (what most people nowadays call God). This dispensation (also called a law, as the type that Moses received on Mount Sinai) can be thought of as a formula for enlightenment or union with the divine, the source of all creation. I want to emphasize that the new dispensation doesn't negate the old one. This is what Christ meant in Matthew 5:17 when he announced that he didn't come to do away with the law but to fulfill it. The formulas employed before remain effective; it's just that the new dispensation is designed to broaden our understanding of the Prime Mover and enhance our relationship to it.

> ANGELS AND ARCHANGELS ARE THE INTELLIGENCES AND ENERGIES BEHIND THE SYMBOLS OF THE STARS, NO MATTER WHAT YOU CHOOSE TO CALL THEM.

Another way to understand the evolution of these dispensations is through the stars—specifically via the zodiac (or, as it's called in the book of Job, the *Mazzaroth*). In the time on Earth when the sun rose in Taurus during the equinox, the formula for divine union utilized polytheism and was based on the symbol of the bull. For example, the highest god in the Sumerian pantheon of the time—Anu—was referred to as the "bull of heaven." Kings of the time typically wore crowns adorned with horns.

Next in the precession came the age of Aries, the ram. During this period, monotheism began to rise in the form of Judaism. The importance of ram horns is still seen today in Jewish rituals. The premium placed on Aries is illustrated in the story of Moses coming down the mountain and getting upset at people worshipping the golden calf (a symbol of Taurus, the older eon). Judaism was also a moon-based system, and Moses was little more than a new version of the ancient Sumerian god of the moon, Sin. Note that Moses received the new law on Mount *Sin*ai (the Temple of the Moon), and Jewish places of worship are known as *syn*agogues.

Next came the age of Pisces, which cemented the role of monotheism in the form of Christianity and Islam. The people of this period no longer used the terminology of *gods* but of *angels*. Christianity in particular is a solar religion (replacing a lunar one)—Jesus is an embodiment of the sun, whereas his twelve disciples are the constellations of the zodiac.

All these ancient dispensations can still be used effectively today in the age of Aquarius, provided you possess the key to understanding them. The key is a familiarity with celestial energies. Without that, much understanding of the old formulas is little more than superstition. Angels and archangels are the intelligences and energies behind the symbols of the stars, no matter what you choose to call them. Gods, deities, stars, angels . . . all of these are merely culturally determined labels. What actually matters is the power that lies behind those labels.

Another way to understand the evolution of these dispensations is through the Middle Pillar (a practice referred to in *High Magick*) and the Tree of Life (discussed in the previous chapter). Essentially, each stage of development is meant to carry us up to the next sphere. The polytheistic eon of Taurus was the very bottom of the tree, Malkuth. Next came Aries—monotheism, Judaism, and all of Judaism's ties to the moon and the ancient god Sin. It's here where humanity entered the sphere of Yesod. Christ introduced the eon of Pisces, in which we traded a lunar-based formula for a solar one and entered Tiphareth. In the age of Aquarius, we move up to the hidden sphere of Da'ath (often given the same attributes as Binah, the sphere of judgment and karma) and a notably Saturnian time of judgment.

I want to reemphasize that the formula of each eon is validly meant to provide humanity with a new dispensation for reaching the abode of the *Empyrean*, or "mind of God," although most early Christian theologians used this term to refer to the dwelling place of God—the divine firmament itself. I have come to favor *Empyrean* instead of the term *God*, simply because the latter carries so much baggage and thousands of years of inherited ideas attached to it. Unlike the magick of older formulas that relied heavily on Judeo-Christian imagery and terminology (for example, God as father), magicians of the eon of Aquarius will move beyond the usage of solar iconography and speak instead of the stars.

The following catalog of angelic correspondences to celestial energies is by no means complete. Furthermore, the suggested reasons for invocation are just a starting point for the countless ways these intelligences can be contacted and summoned. In fact, I've found that you can invoke almost any angel or archangel to fulfill any purpose and get results; it's just that the end result will manifest in radically different ways—an angel corresponding to the energy of Scorpio, for example, will offer protection in a wildly different way than would an angel associated with Gemini.

These lists come from a variety of sources, some of which have been forgotten through time. For example, no one knows who came up with the practice of invoking seventy-two angels for the Shem Operation or how they discovered these energies in the first place— we just know that working with the angels and archangels of the zodiac in this way works. Furthermore, I want to say that I continue to rely on the work of a few other magicians whose knowledge I trust for appropriate correspondences and associations. I highly recommend the work of Damon Brand, an amazing magician who belongs to a group of people known collectively as the Gallery of Magick. His books *The 72 Angels of Magick* and *Archangels of Magick* have proved useful to me in a number of ways. Additionally, Silver RavenWolf's *Angels: Companions in Magick* and Gustav Davidson's *A Dictionary of Angels* have both proved indispensable to me as I explore my own path to working with these energies.

THE TWELVE ARCHANGELS OF THE ZODIAC

MALKIDAEL, ARCHANGEL OF ARIES

The wheel of the zodiac begins with the sign of Aries, which lasts from March 21 through April 19. The archangel who presides over the energy of this period is Malkidael, one of the fiercest warriors of the celestial army. Just as he is first among the zodiacal signs, so is Malkidael the first to rush into battle or to help with any form of strife.

Keys to Visualizing Malkidael of Aries

- Red robes
- Holds a spear and wears a Spartan-like helmet
- Associated with the scent of dragon's blood

Some Reasons to Invoke Malkidael of Aries

- To overcome fear
- For strength and determination during trying times
- To deal with any kind of strife—personal, work-related, spiritual, and the like
- For increased physical strength and stamina
- For hunting of any type (animals, bargains, etc.)

ASMODEL, ARCHANGEL OF TAURUS

The second sign of the zodiac is Taurus, which runs from April 20 through May 20. The energy of Taurus is that of the element of earth, which makes it excellent for any kind of prosperity or agricultural magick. The archangel that presides over this sign is Asmodel. He and the angels of Taurus under his command are known to be some of the most powerful of the zodiac, much like the bull that symbolizes this sign. Asmodel may not be the first to act, or the fastest, but once set in motion he is unstoppable.

Keys to Visualizing Asmodel of Taurus
- Orange-red robes
- Holds a horn of plenty
- Associated with the scent of patchouli

Some Reasons to Invoke Asmodel of Taurus
- For gardening or growing plants of any sort
- To obtain money that is owed to you, or to aid any plan that involves wealth
- To magnetize a long-term career
- To foster patience, persistence, and consistency in any endeavor

Ⅱ

AMBRIEL, ARCHANGEL OF GEMINI

The third sign of the zodiac is Gemini, which begins on May 21 and ends on June 20. The archangel who presides here is Ambriel, the great communicator. As such, his energy is greatly entwined with technology in the modern age, especially social media and the internet. Ambriel can help us understand and articulate abstract concepts to others in a way that their minds can grasp. He is the patron archangel of writers, public speakers, and computer programmers—all people who are immersed in the business of sharing and disseminating knowledge.

Keys to Visualizing Ambriel of Gemini

- Orange robes emblazoned with the symbol of Gemini in darker orange upon them
- Associated with the scent of orange

Some Reasons to Invoke Ambriel of Gemini

- When studying for exams of any sort, in order to retain the information you're learning
- To protect technological devices, such as phones and computers (or even to help make the internet run faster and more efficiently)
- When writing anything from books to posts on the internet
- Any time you wish people to understand the underlying ideas beneath your words
- To facilitate communication between partners, whether they be business or romantic
- To promote your work or gain publicity for any endeavor

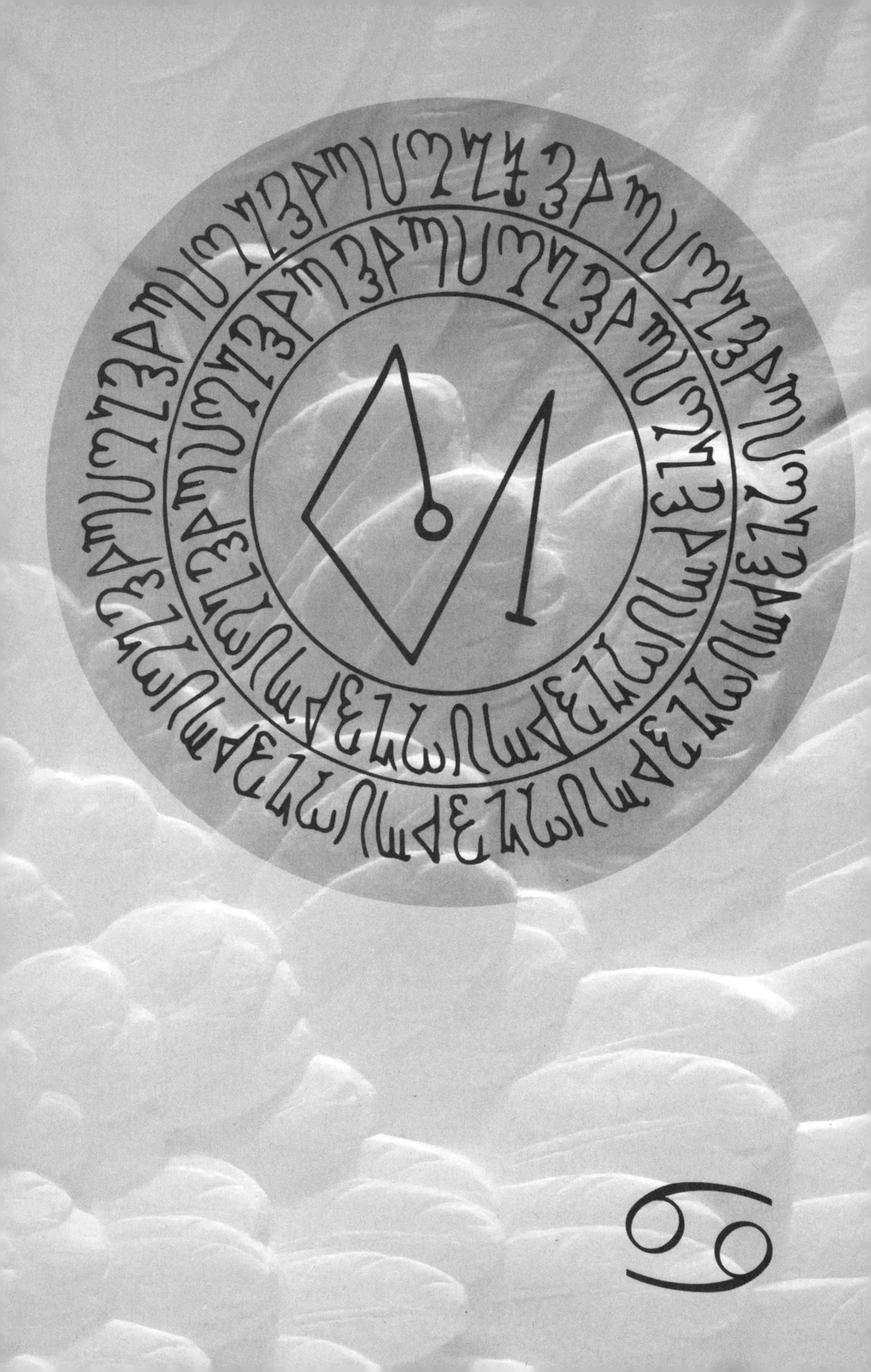

MURIEL, ARCHANGEL OF CANCER

Next up on the zodiacal wheel is the sign of Cancer, which runs from June 21 to July 22. Cancer is one of the three water signs of the zodiac, and it pertains specifically to our home and emotional life. The archangel that presides over this sign is Muriel. She is concerned with making our living environment as stable and comfortable as possible, so that we have a foundation that enables us to pour ourselves wholeheartedly into our work.

Keys to Visualizing Muriel of Cancer
- Dark amber robes emblazoned with the sign of Cancer in dark yellow
- Associated with the scents of jasmine or chamomile

Some Reasons to Invoke Muriel of Cancer
- To secure a new home
- To heal from heartache and gain emotional comfort
- To watch over and protect family members
- To increase intuition
- To improve chances of pregnancy
- To banish and defend against people who are emotionally abusive
- For anything needed in the home, especially anything that promotes an atmosphere of contentment

VERCHIEL, ARCHANGEL OF LEO

The next season after Cancer is Leo. It begins on July 23 and ends on August 22. One of three fire signs, Leo's energy is the most selfless of the zodiac—the epitome of compassion and loyalty. The archangel who presides over Leo is Verchiel. Verchiel is another archangel of victory and success, and therefore can be called upon in any instance where we want to tip the odds in our favor.

Keys to Visualizing Verchiel of Leo

- Gold or yellow robes with a golden breastplate
- Associated with various scents: frankincense, cinnamon, orange, and lemon

Some Reasons to Invoke Verchiel of Leo

- To stay optimistic in dark times
- To send assistance to anyone, whether they be friend or stranger
- For help with accomplishing any substantial task (for example, running a marathon or writing a book)
- For general assistance to help make anything go a little more smoothly

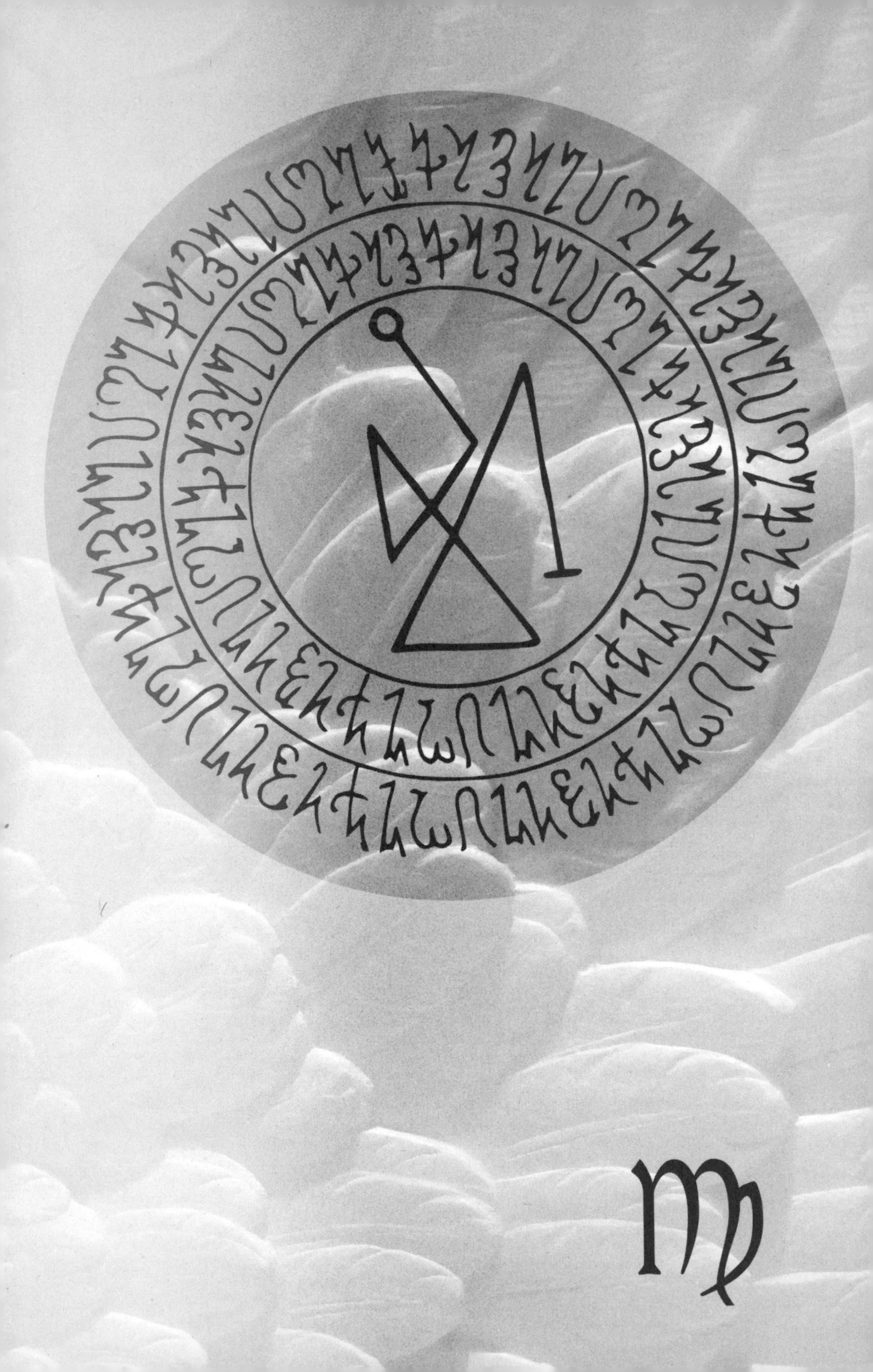

HAMALIEL, ARCHANGEL OF VIRGO

August 23 until September 22 is the period when the energy of Virgo is prominent. Virgo corresponds with intellectual pursuits and solving problems of any size. The archangel of Virgo is Hamaliel, and she is especially affiliated with surgeons and doctors, although she is also known to have an affinity for those involved with magick.

Keys to Visualizing Hamaliel of Virgo

- Yellow-green robes emblazoned with a darker green symbol of Virgo
- Associated with the scents of lavender, lemon balm, and cypress

Some Reasons to Invoke Hamaliel of Virgo

- To assist anyone involved with surgeries or other medical procedures, whether they be doctors or patients
- To receive fair treatment in any situation where you feel as if you're being taken advantage of
- For help understanding complex magickal practices
- For assistance in working toward any goal, but especially those that involve prosperity

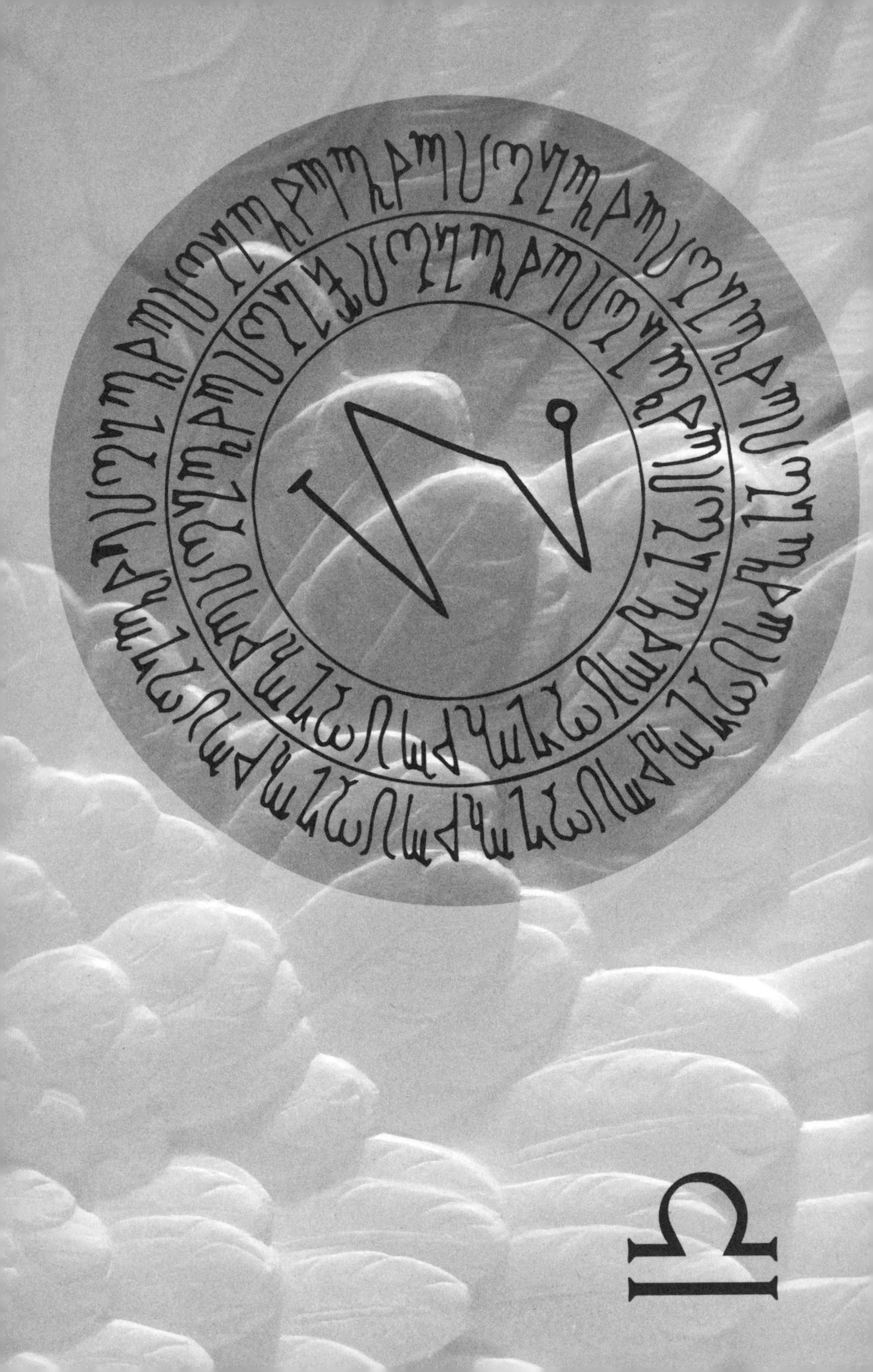

ZURIEL, ARCHANGEL OF LIBRA

Libra season is from September 23 to October 22. The main concern of the energy of Libra is to make certain that all is fair, which is why this sign is symbolized by a scale. Also, the harvest season in the Western Hemisphere usually begins in Libra, and harvests are the very embodiment of plenty. The archangel who presides over this sign and all that pertains to it is Zuriel, who is known for bringing order to chaos.

Keys to Visualizing Zuriel of Libra

- Emerald-green robes
- Holds a scale
- Associated with the scents of chamomile, sweet grass, sweet pea, and tuberose

Some Reasons to Invoke Zuriel of Libra

- To discover hidden enemies
- For help in ridding your home or office of clutter
- To help in any situation in which you feel you or others are being discriminated against
- For help in reaching a mutually beneficial agreement with someone

♏

BARCHIEL, ARCHANGEL OF SCORPIO

The season of Scorpio begins on October 23 and ends on November 21. Scorpio is a water sign and therefore deals primarily with the emotional plane, but it also extends into the realm of psychic intuition and sexuality. The archangel of this sign is Barchiel, who presides over all mystical subjects and things related to the occult.

Keys to Visualizing Barchiel of Scorpio

- Blue-green robes with the sign of Scorpio in darker green
- Associated with the scents of dragon's blood and lotus

Some Reasons to Invoke Barchiel of Scorpio

- To enhance sexual pleasure and assist with issues of repressed sexuality
- To interpret dreams
- To master any form of divination
- To discover the truth about any situation
- To defend against anyone who would attack you for your beliefs

ADNACHIEL, ARCHANGEL OF SAGITTARIUS

Sagittarius season is from November 22 to December 21. This is the sign of poets, philosophers, writers, teachers, and priests. It embodies the energy of potential, growth, and expansion. Those born under this sign never think twice about being honest, even if it wounds the listener. The archangel who governs this sign is Adnachiel. I'm not going into them in much detail here, but if you're familiar with what astrologists call planetary energies, Adnachiel is complementary to Jupiter and can be called upon in any ritual that employs that particular energy (for example, fortune, growth, and prosperity).

Keys to Visualizing Adnachiel of Sagittarius
- Blue robes
- Holds a bow
- Associated with the scents of nutmeg and clove

Some Reasons to Invoke Adnachiel of Sagittarius
- For aid in accomplishing any substantial task, especially if it will enhance your reputation
- For assistance in traveling and experiencing new places
- To increase enjoyment and excitement in your life
- For greater prosperity and wealth
- To overcome any restrictions keeping you from achieving your full potential
- To achieve fame for your talents and abilities

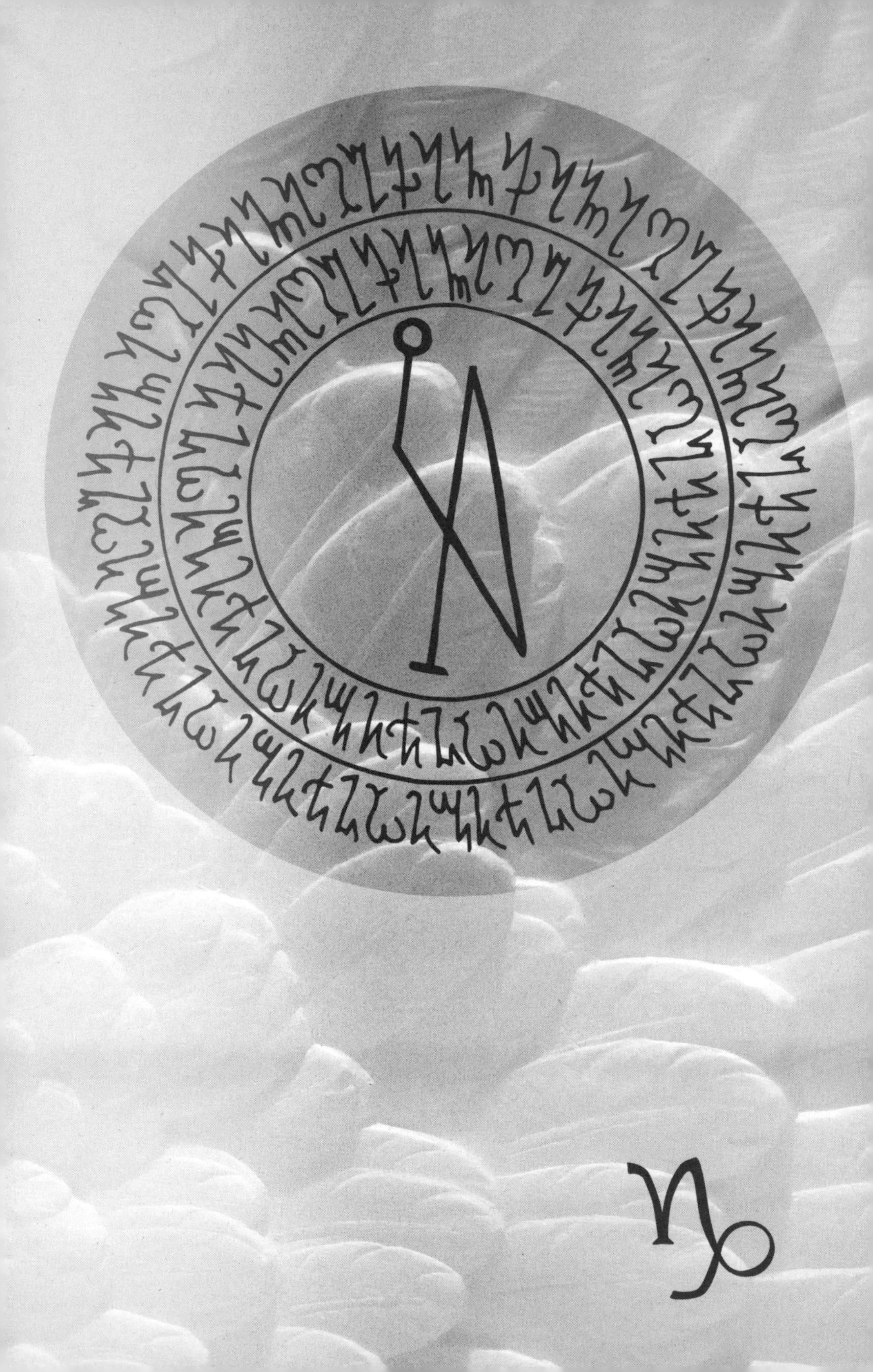

HANAEL, ARCHANGEL OF CAPRICORN

December 22 to January 19 is the season of Capricorn. As an earth sign, Capricorn energy tends to be one of the most grounded of the zodiac, and it's incredibly beneficial when attempting to manifest prosperity. The archangel who rules Capricorn energy is Hanael, who has the feel of a very grounded, traditionally oriented businessperson.

Keys to Visualizing Hanael of Capricorn
- Indigo robes marked with the sign of Capricorn
- Associated with the scents of patchouli and myrrh

Some Reasons to Invoke Hanael of Capricorn
- To assist in any accounting matter
- To influence a business owner in any way
- To receive a fair deal in financial matters
- To protect your business

KAMBRIEL, ARCHANGEL OF AQUARIUS

Between January 20 and February 18 is the season of Aquarius. It embodies the energy of communication, through which we build and maintain connections with others. This endeavor is the specialty of Kambriel, the archangel who rules over this sign. By connecting with others, we build a web of energy that allows us to do more than we would be able to accomplish on our own. The end result of these connections is the sharing of knowledge for the highest good of humanity. Any substantial accomplishment typically involves working together and communicating to make it happen.

Keys to Visualizing Kambriel of Aquarius
- Violet robes emblazoned with the sign of Aquarius
- Associated with the scents of grapefruit and vanilla

Some Reasons to Invoke Kambriel of Aquarius
- For assistance in joining a group or club
- To create harmony between people or within your own life
- To get the word out about a project you want to launch
- To find friends with common interests
- For help with the duties of leadership

AMNITZIEL, ARCHANGEL OF PISCES

The season of Pisces occurs between February 19 and March 20. Since Pisces is the last sign on the zodiacal wheel before it returns to the beginning, this sign is in some ways a vessel that contains elements of all the other signs. For this reason, people born under this sign make excellent magicians. The energy of Pisces is easygoing, fluid, and adaptable. The archangel of Pisces is Amnitziel, who is the intelligence responsible for balancing and harmonizing all of the other signs.

Keys to Visualizing Amnitziel of Pisces
- Crimson robes highlighted by the fish sign in gold
- Associated with various scents: apple, vanilla, myrrh, and juniper

Some Reasons to Invoke Amnitziel of Pisces
- For assistance when using any type of energy healing
- For help when adapting to new situations, environments, and people
- To strengthen any other magick you might be performing
- For blending into the background and remaining unnoticed
- For assistance of any kind

MORE ON PLANETARY ENERGIES

All of the angels and archangels are representations of the intelligences behind celestial phenomena. Just as some are associated with stars, others represent planets. In ancient times, astrologers ascribed seven different planets to represent energies active on the physical plane, each affiliated with a different archangel who was said to rule over and direct that particular form of energy:

- Raphael, archangel of Mercury (represented by the color orange)
- Gabriel, archangel of the moon (purple)
- Anael, archangel of Venus (green)
- Zamael, archangel of Mars (red)
- Sachiel, archangel of Jupiter (blue)
- Michael, archangel of the sun (gold)
- Cassiel, archangel of Saturn (black)

These seven planetary energies were also said to represent different levels of divinity, similar to Dante's presentation in *Paradiso*. Even though it's assumed to be a work of fiction, Dante's descriptions of passing through the various levels of heaven are remarkably similar to what a magician experiences in the process of awakening.

THE SEVENTY-TWO ANGELS OF THE ZODIAC

You'll note that I don't give any visualization cues for the following sets of angels. That's simply because they are best envisioned as smaller, less potent, or vaguer versions of their corresponding archangels. For example, you should visualize all of the angels associated with Aries (Vehuiah, Yeliel, Sitael, Elemiah, Mahasiah, and Lelahel) as lesser versions of Archangel Malkidael. I'm including colors in this list for your convenience, because the simplest way to see these intelligences in your mind's eye is to imagine that they are wearing robes of the corresponding color.

THE ANGELS OF ARIES
The angels of Aries are all associated with the color red.

1.
VEHUIAH
For assistance in developing wisdom, especially
wisdom pertaining to the arts and sciences
For help engaging and completing any difficult task

2.
YELIEL
To defend against unjust attacks by those
who are jealous or malicious
For assistance in experiencing passionate sex

3.
SITAEL
Invoked for protection against wild animals
For help with any kind of adversity
To encourage people to keep their word

4.
ELEMIAH
To rid magicians of troubles that plague their thoughts
To make travels and voyages flow more smoothly

5.

MAHASIAH

To help bring peace to any relationship
For assistance in learning new subjects
quickly and understanding them

6.

LELAHEL

To increase ambition or to help you achieve your ambition
For assistance in gaining fame and fortune within your chosen field

THE ANGELS OF TAURUS

*The angels of Taurus are all associated
with the color reddish-orange.*

7.

ACHAIAH

For patience
To learn any secrets pertaining to nature
For perseverance while undertaking difficult tasks

8.

CAHETEL

To dispel negative energy directed at you from others
To drive away any nonhuman evil entities that seek to cause harm

9.

HEZIEL

To gain the favor of those in positions of power and authority
To ensure that promises made to you are kept

10.

ELADIAH

For help in keeping secrets hidden
To help heal from diseases

11.

LAVIAH

For the power to overcome enemies
To develop fame and renown for a particular talent

12.
HAHAIAH

To gain answers to questions through dreams
For turning enemies into friends

THE ANGELS OF GEMINI

The angels of Gemini are all associated with the color orange.

13.
YEZELEL

To repair damaged friendships or reunite quarreling lovers
To inspire writers

14.
MEBAHEL

For the protection of prisoners
To deliver justice and free the oppressed

15.
HARIEL

To bring peace to any situation

16.
HAKEMIAH

To prevent betrayal and thwart oppressors
To ensure that you are treated with dignity

17.
LAVEL

To help you or others deal with despair, depression, and sorrow
To create music that is emotionally moving

18.
KELIEL

To make you less visible, especially to
anyone intending to do you harm
To make innocence apparent in courts of law

THE ANGELS OF CANCER
The angels of Cancer are all associated with the color yellow.

19.
LOVEL
To inspire love in both friends and enemies
For assistance in making good decisions

20.
PAHALIAH
To help find joy in life
To help "seekers" find the spiritual path most appropriate for them
To assist in the study of religion and theology

21.
NELACHEL
To protect your name against slander
To protect your property against thieves

22.
YEYAYEL
To help bring renown or fame for talents and skills
To get your work known by the general public

23.
MELAHEL
For protection against any type of weapon

24.
CHAHUIAH
To repel insects, rodents, and other vermin
To help in the study of magick

THE ANGELS OF LEO
The angels of Leo are all associated with the color gold.

25.
NETAHIAH
To discover secrets or other forms of hidden information,
which is often revealed during dreams
For the revelation of novel magickal techniques and practices

26.
HAAIAH
For victory in lawsuits and legal matters
To influence politicians, diplomats, and bureaucrats

27.
YERETEL
To deliver one from the hands of enemies
To spread knowledge through writing
To gain fame and recognition to things written

28.
SHAHAHIAH
To protect your health and defend against illnesses
For the required strength and inner peace to
make it through natural disasters

29.
RIYIYEL
To defend against enemies, especially those who may be unseen
To discover the plots and plans of enemies

30.
OMAEL
To help deal with sorrow
To gain patience in difficult times
For help in letting go of past failures and moving on

THE ANGELS OF VIRGO
The angels of Virgo are all associated with the color dark green.

31.
LECAVEL
To help you retain whatever you study
For assistance in passing through crowds unseen

32.
VESHERISH
To defend against untrue accusations,
especially within the court system

33.
YICHUIAH

To discover those who may have betrayed you, or to
thwart the plans of those who are attempting to do so
To aid in manifesting desires in the material realm

34.
LEHACHIAH

To curb anger, both your own and that of others
To bring calm to a situation
To halt the disintegration of a relationship

35.
KEVEKIAH

To regain the friendship or goodwill of someone you have offended
To ensure that something is shared equally

36.
MENADEL

To maintain a job
To protect prisoners

THE ANGELS OF LIBRA
The angels of Libra are all associated with the color pale green.

37.
ANIEL

To communicate with others effectively
To obtain victory without resorting to physical combat

38.
CHAAMIAH

To acquire prosperity
To preserve physical health

39.
REHOEL

For longevity
To heal any form of illness

40.
YEYIZEL

For freedom from imprisonment
To increase psychic intuition
For assistance in the publishing industry

41.
HAHAHEL
To stop the plans of enemies
To prevent slander

42.
MICHEL
To uncover conspiracies
To influence those with political power
To provide safe passage

THE ANGELS OF SCORPIO
The angels of Scorpio are all associated with the color blue-green.

43.
VEVALIAH
To bind or destroy the plans of enemies
For assistance when dealing with a cruel superior

44.
YELAHIAH
To assist in manifesting any desire
To ensure its success, when invoked at the
beginning of any new endeavor

45.
SEALIAH
To repel curses and other forms of negativity directed toward you
To help and comfort those who have been humiliated

46.
ARIEL
To clarify or bring into focus what you truly desire during
times of confusion (often revealed in the form of dreams)

47.
ESHALISH
To make the truth known in any situation
To create love
To receive omens about the future

48.
MIHEL
To ease tensions and strife in a troubled marriage
To increase passion and sensuality

THE ANGELS OF SAGITTARIUS
The angels of Sagittarius are all associated with the color blue.

49.
VEHUEL
To exalt the magician
To humble or dominate any situation that
involves strong personalities
To rise above aggression

50.
DANIEL
For aid in any legal situation

51.
HACHASHISH
To learn the true secret of the Philosopher's
Stone, which elevates the soul

52.
OMEMIAH
For patience and strength while undergoing adversities
To weaken the power of those who would seek to victimize you

53.
NENAEL
To help master a skill, or to teach that skill to another

54.
NITEL
To gain recognition for your art, especially writing of any kind
For long life

THE ANGELS OF CAPRICORN

The angels of Capricorn are all associated with the color indigo.

55.
MIVAHIAH

To help you as a magician win awards and acclaim in your
particular field of interest, or to help someone else do the same
To obtain rightful compensation

56.
POIEL

To obtain any desire

57.
NEMEMIAH

For general prosperity
To help with fatigue

58.
YEYILEL

To ease the pain of sorrow and help the heart to quickly heal
To influence those within the realm of finance

59.
HARACHEL

For help in having a child or matters concerning fertility
For assistance in business dealings

60.
METZEREL

For protection against those who would persecute or bully you

THE ANGELS OF AQUARIUS

The angels of Aquarius are all associated with the color violet.

61.
UMABEL

To obtain friendship
To transform a romantic relationship into a friendship
when you don't share in the other person's feelings

62.
YAYAHEL
To acquire wisdom
For assistance in understanding philosophy
To pass unnoticed through the streets

63.
ANUEL
For a good outcome in any situation involving commerce or banking
To protect a business or make good business deals

64.
MACHIEL
For help in any project involving writing,
especially literature such as novels
To help spread your writing to a wider audience

65.
DAMEBIAH
To ward against malicious magick
For success in any venture that involves being on or near water

66.
MENAKEL
To find any object that has been lost
For the prevention of nightmares

THE ANGELS OF PISCES
The angels of Pisces are all associated with the color crimson.

67.
IYAHEL
For endurance during times of adversity
To break free from any situation in which you feel stuck
To increase fame

68.
CHAVUIAH
To speed up recovery time from illnesses
For assistance in any matter concerning agriculture

69.
RAAHEL
To discover the identity of thieves

70.
YABAMIAH
To find inner peace and a sense of calm in the
middle of chaotic circumstances

71.
HAYIEL
For greater proficiency in magick
To repel harmful magick directed at you by others

72.
MUMIAH
To help ensure success in any endeavor,
especially those involving magick

CHAPTER 4

ANGELS OF THE TAROT

During my research of old resources of the Hermetic Order of the Golden Dawn, I came across references to *angels of the day* and *angels of the night*. This puzzled me for some time, until I realized that day and night were simply pointing to solar/masculine energies and lunar/feminine energies. Accordingly, when invoking these angels, it can be helpful to envision them as being male or female, although please keep in mind that these are merely worldly conventions meant to help you connect with these energies. This angelic breakdown is only true of the numbered cards of the minor arcana; each card of the major arcana, as well as the court cards of the minor arcana, are associated with archangels. In part 2 of this book, I'll offer a couple of practices on how to invoke these energies, as well as a couple of ways to charge the tarot cards as talismans or amulets.

SPIRITUAL MATERIALISM

Most of the world's economy is based on the appetites of the ego, and nowhere is this more starkly pronounced than in spiritual communities. People truly believe that spending hundreds of dollars for yoga pants, meditation cushions, *malas*, retreats, and crystals—or just putting lots of cash on the donation plate—is somehow correlated with increased spirituality. They believe they can actually buy their way into becoming a better person. Of course, this is just another ploy of the ego, which very much wants you to think of yourself as a better person. The magick community isn't exempt from this way of thinking. Most people who claim to practice magick are only going through the motions; it's just a fashion statement on their part, a way to rebel against their constrained, traditional upbringing. They're far more concerned with how witchy their clothes and jewelry look than they are in developing self-discipline and wisdom. As I note elsewhere, it isn't that the implements and other external spiritual trappings are bad—they can, in fact, be helpful. Having multiple tarot decks, for example, is all fine and good—as long as you're doing the work and actually using them for divination (or for the creation of talismans). Buying magickal implements is easy; practicing magick takes work. The point to this rant is that nothing the ego wants has any inherent benefit in and of itself. Regardless of what you buy, wear, or display around your house, or what teacher you associate with, it's still up to you to do what it takes to rise above the ego—which is the only source of darkness in all of the universe. Doing so takes a lot more than buying cool stuff from your local New Age shop.

Please keep in mind that the following catalog of suggested reasons for invocation is by no means complete. If a particular card has come to strongly represent something to you that you don't find here or in any other list or book, I encourage you to trust that connection and work with its power in your magick.

It's no mistake that there's an overlap here with the angels and archangels presented in chapter 3, "Angels and Archangels of the Zodiac." For more on the relationship between these presentations of the energies, I highly recommend *Tarot Talismans: Invoke the Angels of the Tarot* by Chic Cicero and Sandra Tabitha Cicero, who were students of the twentieth-century magician and author Israel Regardie and are probably the world's most respected teachers when it comes to traditional magick of this sort. I've found their work to be invaluable in my own practice.

THE ARCHANGELS OF THE MAJOR ARCANA
The Cards, Their Associated Archangels, and Reasons for Charging and Invocation

CARD 0

THE FOOL
RAPHAEL
To banish anxiety and worry
To undertake a journey

CARD 1

THE MAGICIAN
RAPHAEL
To strengthen your magickal ability

CARD 2

THE HIGH PRIESTESS
GABRIEL
To enhance intuition or psychic perception

CARD 3

THE EMPRESS
ANAEL
To have a child, or increase the chances of pregnancy
To improve your connection to nature

CARD 4

THE EMPEROR
MALKHIDAEL
To lead with strength and wisdom
To set healthy boundaries

CARD 5

THE HIEROPHANT

ASMODEL

To obtain a teacher of magick
To improve as a teacher of magick

CARD 6

THE LOVERS
AMBRIEL

To make decisions that will lead you toward
spiritual growth and development
To attract a relationship that will help you develop spiritually

CARD 7

THE CHARIOT
MURIEL
To gain victory or success in any endeavor with strong opposition

CARD 8

STRENGTH
VERKHIEL
To learn to control your emotions in a healthy, nonrepressed way
To develop healthy self-discipline

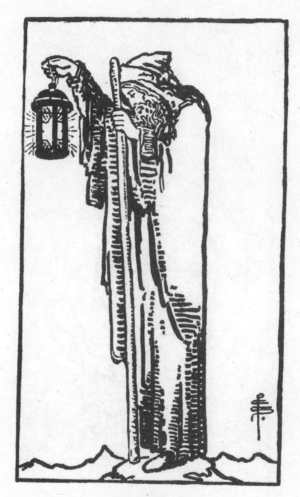

CARD 9

THE HERMIT
HAMALIEL
To increase knowledge, wisdom, and insight

CARD 10

THE WHEEL OF FORTUNE

SACHIEL

To generate good luck
To turn a negative situation around for your benefit

CARD 11
JUSTICE
ZURIEL
To receive success before a judge or to increase the
chances of the judgment being in your favor

CARD 12

THE HANGED MAN

GABRIEL

To gain assistance leaving behind things and habits that
don't benefit you (cigarettes, overeating, gossip, etc.)

CARD 13

DEATH
BARKHIEL
To initiate a change in any situation

CARD 14

TEMPERANCE
ADNAKHIEL
To bring your spiritual life and daily life into harmony and balance

CARD 15

THE DEVIL
HANAEL
To break an addiction

CARD 16

THE TOWER
ZAMAEL

To receive protection
To cause a quick and powerful change

CARD 17

THE STAR
KAMBRIEL
To heal emotional trauma

CARD 18

THE MOON
AMNITZIEL
To banish dishonesty

CARD 19

THE SUN
MICHAEL
To enjoy general happiness and contentment

CARD 20

JUDGMENT
MICHAEL
To begin a new journey in your spiritual practice

CARD 21

THE WORLD
CASSIEL

To experience union with the Empyrean

THE ANGELS AND ARCHANGELS
OF THE MINOR ARCANA
The Cards, Their Associated Angels or Archangels,
and Reasons for Charging and Invocation

SUIT OF WANDS

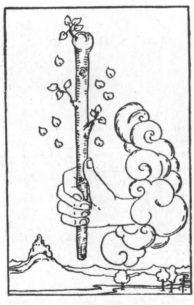 

ACE
ARCHANGEL MICHAEL
To receive courage and strength

2
THE ANGEL OF THE DAY
VEHUEL
THE ANGEL OF THE NIGHT
DANIEL
To begin something new

3

THE ANGEL OF THE DAY
HECHASHIAH

THE ANGEL OF THE NIGHT
AMEMIAH

To set a goal

4

THE ANGEL OF THE DAY
NANAEL

THE ANGEL OF THE NIGHT
NITHAEL

To obtain friends

5

THE ANGEL OF THE DAY
VAHAVIAH

THE ANGEL OF THE NIGHT
YELAYEL

To attain victory in
a confrontation

6

THE ANGEL OF THE DAY
SITAEL

THE ANGEL OF THE NIGHT
ALMIAH

To obtain the respect of
others and gain success

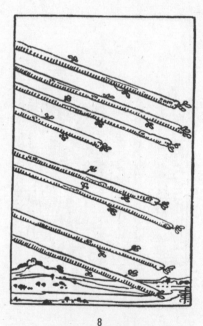

7

THE ANGEL OF THE DAY
MAHASHIAH

THE ANGEL OF THE NIGHT
LELAHEL

To protect your family
and friends

8

THE ANGEL OF THE DAY
NETHAHIAH

THE ANGEL OF THE NIGHT
HAAYAH

To bring quick closure
· to any situation

9

THE ANGEL OF THE DAY
YERATHEL

THE ANGEL OF THE NIGHT
SAAHIAH
To help you prepare for
whatever the future brings

10

THE ANGEL OF THE DAY
REYAYEL

THE ANGEL OF THE NIGHT
UMAEL
To gain some relief from stress
and the weight of your burdens

PAGE
ARCHANGEL MICHAEL
To bless the start of
a new endeavor

KNIGHT
ARCHANGEL MICHAEL
To strengthen other magick
you have performed

QUEEN
ARCHANGEL MICHAEL
To nurture and support
someone else's endeavors
or undertakings

KING
ARCHANGEL MICHAEL
To manage or master anger

SUIT OF CUPS

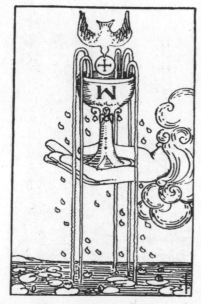

ACE
ARCHANGEL GABRIEL
To open yourself to give
and receive love

2
THE ANGEL OF THE DAY
AYAEL
THE ANGEL OF THE NIGHT
CHAVUYAH
To bless a marriage

3

THE ANGEL OF THE DAY
RAAHEL

THE ANGEL OF THE NIGHT
YEBEMISH

To enjoy and celebrate life,
especially with close friends

4

THE ANGEL OF THE DAY
HAYAYEL

THE ANGEL OF THE NIGHT
MUMIAH

To enhance your appreciation
of the good things you
already have in life

5

THE ANGEL OF THE DAY
LUVAYAH

THE ANGEL OF THE NIGHT
PHAHELIAH

To help cope with loss or
assist in overcoming grief

6

THE ANGEL OF THE DAY
NELAKHEL

THE ANGEL OF THE NIGHT
YEYAYEL

To be able to let go of
the past and move on

7

THE ANGEL OF THE DAY
MELOHEL

THE ANGEL OF THE NIGHT
CHAHAVIAH

To realize your heart's desire

8

THE ANGEL OF THE DAY
VULIAH

THE ANGEL OF THE NIGHT
YELAHIAH

To be able to bring a sense of
closure to past matters and move
on to the next stage of life

9

THE ANGEL OF THE DAY
SAALIAH

THE ANGEL OF THE NIGHT
ERIEL

The "wish card"; use
for anything you are
hoping to manifest

10

THE ANGEL OF THE DAY
ESHELIAH

THE ANGEL OF THE NIGHT
MAYAHEL

To foster success and happiness
for a family member

PAGE
ARCHANGEL GABRIEL
To increase psychic perceptions

KNIGHT
ARCHANGEL GABRIEL
To protect against melancholy

QUEEN
ARCHANGEL GABRIEL
To be more compassionate, or
to bring compassion to another

KING
ARCHANGEL GABRIEL
To master your emotions
without repressing them

SUIT OF SWORDS

ACE
ARCHANGEL RAPHAEL
To develop single-
pointed concentration

2
THE ANGEL OF THE DAY
YEZALEL
THE ANGEL OF THE NIGHT
MEBAHEL
To bring an end to
constant worrying

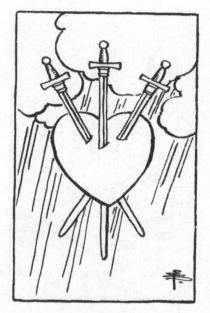

3

THE ANGEL OF THE DAY
HARIEL

THE ANGEL OF THE NIGHT
HAQAMIAH

To heal yourself or someone
else from emotional damage

4

THE ANGEL OF THE DAY
LEVAYAH

THE ANGEL OF THE NIGHT
KELIEL

To overcome insomnia

5

THE ANGEL OF THE DAY
ENIEL

THE ANGEL OF THE NIGHT
CHAAMIAH

To let go of an argument
To break emotional attachment

6

THE ANGEL OF THE DAY
REHAEL

THE ANGEL OF THE NIGHT
YEYEZEL

To move on from a hurtful past

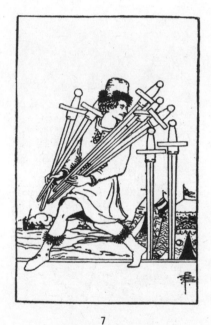

7

THE ANGEL OF THE DAY
HEHAHEL

THE ANGEL OF THE NIGHT
MAYAKHEL

To maintain a secret
or to learn one

8

THE ANGEL OF THE DAY
VEMBAEL

THE ANGEL OF THE NIGHT
YAHOHEL

To see through the constraints
of your own thoughts

9

THE ANGEL OF THE DAY
ANUEL

THE ANGEL OF THE NIGHT
MACHIEL

To banish anxiety

10

THE ANGEL OF THE DAY
DAMBAYAH

THE ANGEL OF THE NIGHT
MENEQEL

To accept an end to something
To bring an end to something

PAGE
ARCHANGEL RAPHAEL
To begin a stimulating
intellectual pursuit

KNIGHT
ARCHANGEL RAPHAEL
To gain the ability to face a
difficult situation head on

QUEEN
ARCHANGEL RAPHAEL
To enhance wisdom

KING
ARCHANGEL RAPHAEL
To ensure fair treatment
in a given situation

SUIT OF PENTACLES

ACE
ARCHANGEL URIEL
To manifest something
in the material realm

2
THE ANGEL OF THE DAY
LEKHABEL
THE ANGEL OF THE NIGHT
VESHIRIAH
To help balance finances or time

3

THE ANGEL OF THE DAY
YECHAVIAH

THE ANGEL OF THE NIGHT
LEHACHIAH

To increase the appreciation
of your craft in the
eyes of superiors

4

THE ANGEL OF THE DAY
KUQIAH

THE ANGEL OF THE NIGHT
MENADEL

To banish greed
To increase protection

5

THE ANGEL OF THE DAY
MIBAHAYAH

THE ANGEL OF THE NIGHT
PUYAEL

To eliminate poverty or
poverty mentality

6

THE ANGEL OF THE DAY
NEMAMIAH

THE ANGEL OF THE NIGHT
YEYELEL

To earn good karma
To increase generosity

7

THE ANGEL OF THE DAY
HERACHEL

THE ANGEL OF THE NIGHT
MITZRAEL

To increase favor in finances

8

THE ANGEL OF THE DAY
AKAYAH

THE ANGEL OF THE NIGHT
KEHETHEL

To focus and heighten
self-discipline

9

THE ANGEL OF THE DAY
HAZIEL

THE ANGEL OF THE NIGHT
ELDAYAH

To increase self-sufficiency

10

THE ANGEL OF THE DAY
LAVIAH

THE ANGEL OF THE NIGHT
HIHAAYAH

To gain prosperity

PAGE
ARCHANGEL URIEL
To learn or begin a
new field of study

KNIGHT
ARCHANGEL URIEL
To gain perseverance
and steadfastness

QUEEN
ARCHANGEL URIEL
To thoroughly enjoy your
material possessions instead of
dwelling on what you lack

KING
ARCHANGEL URIEL
To master the art of manifesting

PART 2

PRACTICES AND
RITUALS

Before we transition fully into the practice-oriented portion of this book, I want to say a little bit more about manifestation, how magick works, and how to enhance the efficacy of your practice, whether it be more focused in meditation or centered in ritual and ceremony. This distinction—meditation versus ritual—might not initially seem important, but in my experience, most people gravitate more toward one or the other. I had ample time to explore both when I was on death row, and the practices you'll find here are the result of those nearly two decades of intense devotion and experimentation. I encourage you to try out all these techniques for a period of time before deciding what works best for you.

I also want to recognize that I often use the words *practice* and *ritual* interchangeably, and maybe lean on the former term a little bit more as a general catch-all. However, as you'll find in the chapters to come, what I'm officially labeling as *rituals* here are typically quite a bit more involved, whereas *practices* can often be simple and quick.

ATTITUDE AND MANIFESTATION

Some people think that manifestation is simply a matter of putting enough energy into an imprint on the etheric or astral level of reality until it eventually catches in some way on the physical realm. This can be true, but what most people don't comprehend when doing practical magick is that the thing they're trying to manifest is already theirs but hasn't been unearthed yet. Manifestation simply means that something has finally been freed from the psychic muck and karma it's been buried under, which is one reason that energy work is so necessary in magick. Whether our efforts at manifestation meet with success or not depends on a number of factors, but one thing I have found to be incredibly important is to adopt a sense of completion after a ritual. We must believe as much as possible that the desired result of our practical magick has already been accomplished. Moving through our day as if it's already a done deal will significantly increase the chances that it is, because magick is always empowered by the faith we put into it.

> MAGICK IS ALWAYS EMPOWERED BY THE FAITH YOU PUT INTO IT.

Unfortunately, most people go through life with a profound sense of lack. That poverty mentality carries over into their magick, which makes it a lot more difficult for them to feel as if things are already manifested in the desired way. Interestingly, some evangelical Christians have the right attitude about prayer and manifestation. I once heard a TV preacher refer to what he called "living in a state of joyous expectation." He advised his congregation to foster the feeling that their prayers had already been answered, asserting that this would make it far more likely that they would be. This is precisely how magick works. If you're fretting every five minutes or so about whether or not your magick is working, the chances are that it isn't and won't. Basically all you're doing is pulling your magick back to you over and over again, and so it never gets the chance to do its work on the material plane. It's far more effective to release your expectations and accept that whatever results come your way are a forgone conclusion.

When it comes to practical magick, people also don't normally consider that our physical bodies and environments are manifestations of a higher self that created these forms for a particular purpose. For this reason, the old adage "Be careful what you wish for" is incredibly important to keep in mind when exploring practical magick. These are extremely potent techniques—another reason why following the 90/10 rule I mentioned in the introduction is incredibly important.

CHAOS MAGICK AND FREE WILL

The first thing I learned from my practice was that I had orchestrated the patterns of my life in a way that was designed to awaken me to the experience of divinity. I realized that not one single thing in my life was a coincidence or mistake, and there never would be. Instead, it was a methodical production designed to promote maximum growth. Produced by who? And if every experience is somehow mapped out, what about free will? Chaos magicians reject the idea of God, and some even assert that the omnipotent creator scenario is merely a parable that refers to the unconscious or subconscious mind. Magick works, therefore, because it triggers changes in the deepest corners of our psyche, and that in turns alters our perception and experience. I think there's truth to this, but I can also see divine orchestration at play in my own life. For example, if I hadn't been falsely accused and put on death row, I never would have had the time or motivation to learn, experiment, and practice magick as I did. In prison, I had no choice—my life depended on it. So, a situation that looks terrible and hellish from the outside is the very thing that led to the most positive results.

QUANTUM PHYSICS AND MAGICK

Science as it currently stands is a patchwork of scraps of information, and only recently—with the advent of quantum physics—has it offered a cohesive understanding of the mechanics of the universe. Magicians have been exploring this topic for thousands of years, but they typically have lacked a secular vocabulary to describe the process and practice of magick. Now modern science is beginning to provide that vocabulary.

Quantum physics asserts that we exist within a unified matrix of energy, and one of the primary laws of this matrix is quantum entanglement. Quantum entanglement stipulates that all things that have been physically linked remain connected on an energetic level, even if they become separated by vast distances. Prior to the big bang, all matter, space, and time were condensed into an infinitely small, dense point—it wasn't just that everything was in direct contact with everything else; nothing was separate. This means that the atoms composing the molecules involved in the neurotransmitters associated with the thoughts you're having right now as you read this are in immediate contact with the tiniest particles in stars trillions of light years away. When it comes right down to it, we are all stars—a basic aspect of reality that underlies many of the forthcoming practices.

"AS ABOVE, SO BELOW; AS WITHIN, SO WITHOUT"

"As above, so below; as within, so without"—I believe these to be the greatest and most profound words ever uttered in the history of magick. They're a blueprint of how the universe is constructed, but also an operator's manual—concise instructions on how to manifest our desires. Everything we witness in the physical world is also mirrored in the energetic (or astral) realm, the subtler planes of existence studied by magicians and quantum theorists alike.

The matter and space that compose us are entangled on a quantum level with the matter and space of everything else that can be said to exist. One implication of this is that by causing a change in ourselves, we also cause a change in the remainder of the external universe—a truism put to the test by magicians for thousands of years and more recently by the World Peace Group in their "Super Radiance" studies that examined the tangible effects of group meditation on greater society.[1] In short, what the World Peace Group documented is that war-related deaths and violent crime rates dropped, even when the experiment was conducted multiple times and other factors were statistically controlled. They also found that the positive effects increased dramatically the more trained meditators there were involved in the experiment.

EXPERIMENTATION

I'm not a traditional magician by any means. If you've read *High Magick*, you're already aware of the importance I place on finding your own way with these practices. When I was exploring practical magick on death row, I originally believed that you had to perform the daily rituals by the book. About a year or so into it, however, I gradually began to test how much time and energy to put into something to make it stronger and more effective. I made certain tweaks to get better results and took extensive records of my work. I encourage you to do the same, because keeping track of your alterations to the traditional techniques is essential to a magician's learning process.

> **MAGICK IS LIKE ANYTHING ELSE—YOU GET OUT OF IT WHAT YOU PUT INTO IT.**

The first important change I made was in the amount of time I put into each exercise. For example, after you memorize the basics, the Lesser Banishing Ritual of the Pentagram (LBRP) can be completed in about five minutes. I first extended this to twenty or thirty minutes, mostly by increasing the number of inhalations when tracing the pentagrams around me.

But I also spent more time visualizing the pentagrams flaming around me in each of the four cardinal directions, seeing them grow brighter and brighter each time I inhaled. Then I tried this same type of extension when invoking the archangels, not rushing the visualizations but really taking my time vibrating their names. Right away I found that it made their presence a lot more tangible.

The main thing I came to understand is that finishing a particular ritual isn't the end goal. When I made each step as strong as possible, I began to see greater benefit from what I considered to be the simplest of techniques. I quickly found out that magick is like anything else—you get out of it what you put into it. For this reason, a devoted beginner can see better results than a stickler magician who's been practicing for years and years.

That said, I'll emphasize again how important it is to decrease your attachment to results. Just focus on performing each step as sincerely and thoroughly as possible and try to forget about the outcomes you want to happen.

MAGICKAL TOOLS AND IMPLEMENTS

Experimentation also comes into play when it comes to the external forms of your practice. When I was in prison, I had no choice but to employ what some call the *empty-hand technique*—that is, magick without the tools and implements that most apprentices use from day one (for example, wands, incense, candles, pictures, and so on). When you follow the traditional approach, you accumulate a lot of props over the years, and for the longest time that's how I thought of these things—as mere props.

A friend of mine recently told me that he was having trouble with his practice. "I want to believe in magick," he said, "but I just can't seem to make the leap from *wanting* to believe to actually believing." I think this struggle is common for most people—they have trouble convincing the psyche that they're actually performing magick. For these people, tools can be incredibly important. The implements create a type of distraction that keeps their conscious mind occupied while they actively train their unconscious to respond positively to the prop. Eventually whatever tools they're using contribute to the belief that they're actually doing magick.

That said, if you can't perform magick without tools, it can be quite limiting. Imagine being a Buddhist who can only practice meditation if they have handy their favorite cushion. I didn't have a cushion on death row, and I didn't have any wands or candles—if I had waited to have these things, I never would have survived in there. There were times when I would see the guards torturing some poor clown down the row and I knew it was only a matter of minutes before they got to me. I had to learn to calm and center myself and start invoking angels and archangels in situations where fear was so thick in the air you could barely breathe. This is the atmosphere that led me to feel strongly that a magician should be able to be dropped off naked in a jungle on the other side of the world and still be able to perform incredibly powerful magick.

ANYONE CAN CHARGE A TALISMAN OR TOOL FOR THEIR OWN PURPOSES AND USE IT TO AFFECT OTHERS.

I've only recently started using tools. Specifically, I've collected a wand for banishing, a wand for invoking, yet another wand to direct energy when I'm circumambulating, a chalice to represent the element of water, and—my latest obsession—lots of incense. I burn frankincense and eat the resin regularly, collecting the ashes in a silver chalice that's accumulating energy on my shrine. When the chalice gets full, I plan to take it to Central Park and scatter the ashes so that they become part of the earth here. I want people to interact with that energy and experience the protection, guidance, and illumination of the practices associated with the frankincense I've employed in my rituals. In similar fashion, my wands will eventually dissolve into smaller components and bless the earth with all the energy and love they've accumulated over the years.

Traditionally, magicians are supposed to craft their own tools, especially wands. Before employing what's called the *Rainbow Wand* for invocations, for example, the magician is instructed to shape the wand, paint it, and then go through the process of consecrating and blessing it with all twelve zodiacal energies. What's actually happening in this process is that a magician is customizing their impact on the universe. For this reason, I've started to get more excited about magickal implements, because they're assisting me in my goal to bring as much divine light to this plane as possible. I now see using physical objects, art pieces, and all sorts of magickal tools as means of sending massive amounts of divine energy into the collective unconscious of all humanity. Charging my wand is just another way of working to awaken all sentient beings.

I'm also employing more tools such as herbs, stones, blessed water, and crystals. I plan on leaving energized pieces of amethyst and quartz throughout the city for people to find—my intention is to raise the vibration of consciousness with each object as much as I possibly can. I find myself being pulled more and more toward alchemy as well, specifically in the form of tinctures and spagyrics (alcohol and herb mixtures that have been charged with energy). For example, right now I'm working on a tincture to embody the planetary energy of the sun—the energy of health, vitality, victory, success, and happiness. Over the next month, as the frankincense resin slowly dissolves in alcohol, I'll perform an entire Sol invocation ritual, complete with the appropriate archangels and angels. I'll circumambulate the temple hundreds of times, build up as much chi as possible, then push it all into the tincture. It takes about three hours to do the entire exercise. After a month of daily practice, all I have to do is place a few drops of that tincture under my tongue and swallow while focusing on a particular intention.

The point is that anyone can charge a talisman or tool for their own purposes and use it to affect others. Someone who has no experience with magick at all could use them as easily as someone with a lifetime of practice under their belt. For example, since happiness is one of the qualities associated with the energy of the sun, I could place a couple drops of the tincture I'm talking about under my own tongue or in a friend's cup of tea. It might help to hold the intention of happiness in my mind while doing so, but the energy I've placed into the tincture works whether or not my friend is conscious of my original intention.

YOUR ALTAR

Finally, I want to say a little bit about how to personalize your altar. Although having an altar isn't necessary, some people like to have one in the center of the space where they prefer to perform their regular practices of magick. In traditional ceremonial magick, altars are quite plain—just a black square of some type. That color and shape are representative of the material world, so employing them in your magick helps your manifestation efforts on the physical plane. In fact, to this day, I still use a black square.

As I've encouraged you to do elsewhere, please find what works best for you. If you want to use an altar, it could be a desk, a folding card table, a tapestry or cloth of some sort, or anything else you feel connected to. Just make sure that whatever it is fits the space where you want to do your magick and that your space isn't too cluttered to work in. Mine just holds my regular tools—the wands and chalice I mentioned above, a pentacle, and an incense burner.

Wherever you place your altar (as well as what you put upon it) will become saturated with the energy of your magick over time. I recommend keeping this in mind when deciding where to situate your altar at home.

CHAPTER 5

MIND TRAINING, MINDFULNESS, AND MEDITATION

Often when people hear the words *mindfulness* and *meditation*, they automatically start thinking about Eastern practices that seem boring and to have very little to do with the exciting rituals involved with ceremonial magick. In actuality, meditation and mind training are critically important to your development as a magician—a ritual's success depends on them. The magician and author John Michael Greer once said that everyone he knows who has made any real progress in magick has also had a background in some form of meditation.[1] Additionally, in traditional magick, magicians are expected to familiarize themselves with different meditative states and attain the ability to enter them effortlessly. Even beginning practitioners of magick need to be able to narrow their focus and concentrate in the middle of whatever chaos is happening around them. Doing so can make all the difference when it comes to the efficacy of your magick. Meditation also has the benefit of helping you let go of expectations in your practice—expectations that can lead to a lot of needless doubt and impatience.

I've practiced meditation for about half my life now—traditional zazen sitting meditation, working with koans, energy circulation . . . you name it. Every type of meditation has its own benefits, but the form of meditation I've experienced the most results from is what I call *prison cell meditation*. It's a shortcut to enter a state of single-pointed concentration, transcend the self, and merge with the divine. I practice this meditation every time I'm alone and have a few moments to spare, such as when I'm traveling on the subway or going to the gym. The more I practice it, the more powerful and noticeable its effects are on my psyche. I first came across some version of the following in *The Mystical Qabalah* by the magician Dion Fortune.

PRACTICE: **PRISON CELL MEDITATION**

Imagine that you're standing in the middle of the floor of a prison cell. Around you are solid concrete walls and a solid steel door. The only window is a small slit on the back wall of your cell, but it's so high up above your head that you can't see out of it unless you grip the ledge and haul yourself up with sheer brute strength. Imagine that you pull yourself up there by your fingertips, actually feeling what it would be like—the muscles in your hands, forearms, and biceps all activated and getting more exhausted by the second; the rough texture of the wall scraping your belly and thighs as you struggle to ascend; the cold steel of the window bars around your hands.

When you finally pull yourself up above the ledge, you're nearly blinded by a brilliant light from the outside. It's the light of creation, and it bursts into the window and makes everything disappear. There's only the light—no prison cell, no window, and no you. Nothing exists anymore but infinite light.

That's the meditation. Just like the pull-up or chin-up you're imagining yourself doing, one repetition is probably not enough to do much. There aren't any rules as to how many times you should visualize the above, but I think ten reps is a good start. And when that becomes easy, try working your way up to a hundred times. When you get truly proficient at it, you'll notice a peculiar sensation. As you imagine the light obliterating everything (including you), you'll start to feel as if you've been cast back into your own body—gently, yet forcefully. You'll also experience a temporary state of being grounded in the present moment, in your physical form, with no stray thoughts whatsoever.

Mindfulness has been increasing in popularity for the last decade or so, and people apply it in the context of just about anything these days—golf, cooking, running, tennis, parenting, and so on. Originating thousands of years ago in Eastern traditions (namely, Buddhism and Hinduism and their predecessors), mindfulness is a form of meditation that refers to the act of bringing our attention back to the present moment, over and over again. For those who haven't practiced mindfulness, it can sound incredibly easy or insignificant, but most people who give it a try find it a lot more difficult and rewarding than my description makes it sound.

One reason that mindfulness has become widespread is its documented benefits for body and mind. There's a ton of literature out there (thousands of studies now) on how and why it improves brain chemistry and reduces stress, so I won't go into the science behind why mindfulness is so effective. I'd like to give you my own take, however, because it might be useful to you later on, when it comes to the advanced techniques.

EVERYTHING IS MADE OF ENERGY

Everything that is made of energy has a vibrational frequency, and everything is made of energy—people, places, things, even consciousness. Different energies have different vibrational rates. Our consciousness is only capable of interacting with energies close to our own. This is why sports fans tend to hang out with one another, people of a given political party don't typically interact with those who belong to others, and people in general stay within exclusive social circles. If those we come in contact with aren't resonating at the same frequency as we are, they usually pass from our lives fairly quickly.

Because everything is made of energy—including our thoughts—and magick is about shaping and using energy, then it follows that we'd want to be more aware of that energy and the ways in which it manifests. Unfortunately, our minds are rarely fully focused on what we're doing or experiencing, especially in today's world. Instead, our consciousness jumps from thought to thought, device to device; it moves from past events to future hopes in the blink of an eye, daydreaming, fantasizing, worrying, and so on. Every time we aren't fully engaged in the present moment, energy is escaping from our aura; we are unconsciously discharging it into manifesting life situations we probably never wanted in the first place.

For example, when we constantly go over worries in our head, what we're actually doing is feeding energy into creating situations that will just end up causing us more worry. Thankfully not every thought and emotion we feed energy into manifests in the physical world, but even so, that energy is wasted when it could otherwise be used to create the life we want or fuel our spiritual growth. Mindfulness helps us cultivate the ability to send our energy where we want it to go, as well as refrain from letting it manifest situations and experiences we don't want.

I often repeat the adage "Where attention goes, energy flows." We want our attention to support our growth and progress, not detract from it. When our minds are full of what we're doing right now—how we're feeling and what we're thinking in this moment—then we can be fully present and create a feedback loop that sustains us, as opposed to sending our energy out into whatever random thought and fear happens to be crossing our minds.

PRACTICE: **ZAZEN**

Zazen is the simplest mindfulness practice I know of. For me, it's also been the most difficult. To practice the traditional Japanese form, put a cushion on the floor and kneel on the cushion with your butt touching your heels. Rest your hands in your lap with palms up, one hand on top of the other, with your thumbs touching, almost as if you were holding a giant egg. Keep your eyes open, but gently so, and focus on the floor a couple of feet in front of you. There shouldn't be anything between you and the floor to distract you. Lastly, try not to move (unless, of course, there's some kind of emergency). Just sit up straight and be as still as possible until the session is over.

Now, here's the hard part: Pay attention. Pay attention to your body when it starts to hurt (because it will start to hurt). Pay attention to your thoughts when they happen (because plenty of thoughts are going to happen). Pay attention to your breath as the air comes in and out of your body (that will hopefully happen a lot too).

Actually, the hardest part isn't paying attention—it's paying attention without making judgment calls. This type of meditation isn't about getting it right but rather witnessing whatever happens without making more stories about whatever's happening. So, just pay attention and experience whatever comes up and do your best to come back to the present moment over and over again.

It's harder to do this practice when you first start out. With all the aches and pains and strange thoughts that seem to come out of nowhere, it might even seem impossible. With that in mind, just start with five minutes or so until you get the hang of it. When five minutes seems workable, try ten, then maybe five extra minutes a week until you work your way up to a half hour or so.

CEREMONIAL MAGICK AND THE PRESENT MOMENT

Traditional forms of meditation aren't for everyone. I practiced zazen for years and never experienced a sense of the present moment, but the visualizations and breath work involved with angelic invocations brought me there seemingly right away. Then again, maybe the time I devoted to my sitting practice somehow prepared me for the meditations involved in ceremonial magick. Like I said before, all practice is beneficial in its own way, and if you actually put the time in, you'll find out what works best for you.

The first time I noticed awareness as a benefit of the invocations was on a day when Lorri was scheduled to visit me in prison. I was in my cell getting ready to walk down to the visitation room, and as I was sitting on the edge of my bunk, leaning over to put my shoes on, something felt different about the whole experience. I suddenly realized that I was *right there*—completely in the present moment. I wasn't lacing up my shoes and thinking about something else, I wasn't standing up and traveling somewhere else in my mind—I was exactly right where I was, in my cell, and attentive to every detail of my actions. If you haven't experienced something like this before, it might sound like no big deal, but I personally found it to be incredibly profound.

That was the moment I realized just how much I'd been hijacked by my own ego. Everything the ego does and encourages us to think and feel jettisons us from the present moment like a missile. Our bodies go through the motions, our minds jump around like sugar-fueled children. The present moment is poison to the ego—or the cure, depending on your point of view—because when we're attentive to right here, right now, there's no room for anything else—no wanting the weather to be different, no judging ourselves for not being good enough meditators, no complaining that our partner left the sink full of dishes. Everything is just as it is, and we're just as we are right there with it.

By contrast, the ego can only dwell in the past or the future. It tries to convince us that we're the amalgamation of previous experiences, relationships, dramas, victories, tragedies, and so on. It constantly projects itself into future scenarios of its own creation, where it plays out endless hopes, fears, and expectations. It has to do this constantly, because this is the only way it can assure itself it will survive. For this reason, it will do anything it can to keep us from experiencing the now.

PRACTICE: **NOTICING THE STRATEGIES OF THE EGO**

Find a comfortable spot and sit, stand, or lie there for a couple of minutes. Try to pay attention only to what's happening right now—what your skin feels like, the touch of your breath as it enters and exits your body, the temperature of the air around you, the sounds you hear outside your window, and so on. See what thoughts come to mind as you do this. Don't try to stop your mind from doing what it does, and don't resist whatever the ego is going to throw at you. The point is to simply notice it. Are you thinking about what you're going to eat for dinner? Do you keep remembering something that happened to you yesterday? Do judgments of some sort arise? Whatever it is, just notice it. If nothing comes up in a couple of minutes, try a longer period of time. Eventually the ego will present something interesting enough to remove you from the present moment entirely—often so skillfully that you won't even notice it at first.

The entire reason that we're born into the material realm is to experience it. That seems like a commonsense thing to say, but under the influence of the ego we behave as if we want to be anywhere else but here. One of the main reasons that life can seem so difficult is because we're more invested in resisting it than we are in living it. We fight against our experience constantly, and most people live their entire lives without ever truly experiencing much of it at all. Life gives us situation after situation, inviting us to participate and truly experience each one, and the ego responds by convincing us that things have to be different, that if they were only different we'd be happy, more fulfilled, safe, relaxed, and so on.

Unfortunately, the more we resist, the harder life becomes. That's because the energy we're meant to expend on experiencing the physical realm is going toward unconsciously creating situations that will make it even more difficult to avoid the physical realm. Think about the negative effects that result from any addiction (to alcohol, drugs of any type, social media, etc.) and you'll see this immediately to be true. If we move in the other direction, however—that is, if we become more invested in being awake and present in the moment—life tends to become more interesting, easeful, and poignant. It isn't that life will automatically become brilliant and special at every turn, but I can say from personal experience that if you're more present, the universe and your higher self won't be so interested in throwing hardships at you at every turn.

Buddhist traditions teach that an untrained and unfocused mind produces *dukkha*, a kind of cyclical energy that keeps us trapped in suffering. Some ceremonial magicians teach that dukkha has a type of intelligence behind it called Choronzon (sometimes referred to as the Dweller in the Abyss or the Demon of Dispersion). In some ways, Choronzon is the opposite of an angelic intelligence, and it's Choronzon that stands between us and enlightenment. When the dispersing aspects of this intelligence are highlighted, we can see how it operates much like the ego, doing anything it can to keep us from achieving spiritual awakening, no matter what we call it.

PRACTICE: **ARCHANGEL MEDITATION**

This is a short meditation practice to call up the blessings of different archangels without having to do more elaborate practices such as the LBRP. I recommend beginning with just one archangel and eventually working your way up to six. Let's say you want to add more growth and wealth to your life—I'd recommend doing this meditation with Tzadkiel, the archangel of Chesed.

As you walk around throughout the day, practice paying attention to what you're doing while simultaneously invoking your chosen archangel. If you're sitting at a desk at work, for example, occasionally visualize the archangel expanding in front of you while you inhale. Then exhale (and do the same after every visualization to follow). Then inhale while you imagine the archangel growing incredibly large behind you. Then do the same for your right side, your left, above, and, finally, below you.

When you've gone through this entire sequence, imagine that you're encased in a sphere of the archangel you've invoked. Try doing this once every half hour or so. After you get comfortable using one archangel, try two. Eventually work your way up to six (for example, those described in chapter 1).

The ultimate goal of this exercise is to be able to do it no matter what you're doing during the day. A meditation master would be able to do this in the middle of an intense conversation, without anyone knowing it. This is an excellent practice to train your mind and begin to focus your thoughts upward toward a higher frequency, so to speak. Instead of allowing your consciousness to run amok from one fear or preoccupation to another, you're training your mind upon a divine focus and absorbing the energy associated with archangels in the process.

ANXIETY, FAITH, AND FEAR

Through my own practice I've come to believe that the greatest detriment to our own development is the downward spiral of fear into which we habitually throw ourselves. Modern science is just now beginning to discover and describe the connections between our thought processes and the physical world. Simply put, our thoughts can either improve or harm our physical forms. Anxious or fear-based thoughts are associated with chemicals in our bloodstream that lead to anything from weight gain and high blood pressure to even illnesses, such as shingles. Thoughts of happiness and love, on the other hand, are associated with chemicals that promote feelings of well-being, increased immune function, and so on. I know this firsthand from my experience on death row, especially during my final week in which I was overwhelmed by stress and fear and suffered terrible nausea and canker sores as a result (an experience I refer to in chapter 4 of *High Magick*). This is why some form of mind training or meditation is so important to the magician: it helps us surface those thoughts that are detrimental, become aware of our habitual cognitive patterns, and establish ways of thinking that actually promote what we want out of life.

Don't get me wrong—the macho, stereotypical American male, "no fear" approach to life is the furthest thing from what I'm talking about, mainly because it doesn't work and, in fact, tends to backfire. We simply can't banish our fear by forceful means. When we try to white-knuckle it and battle fear head on, all we're doing is placing more attention on it and helping it grow in strength. We're simply feeding it more energy, thereby assisting it in consuming even more of our thoughts.

Of course, fear goes by many names—anxiety, worry, regret, despair, anger, stress, doubt—and all of us have our own particular way of expressing its fundamental energy. Regardless what we call it, pretty much every unpleasant internal state we experience can be traced back to fear in one way or another, and the only effective way to overcome it is to become aware of its lies and disengage entirely. We do that by employing mindfulness and shifting the focus of our attention toward thoughts grounded in ease, comfort, and love. Doing so, we're able to generate a whole new set of chemicals and positive energy that will bring about changes we actually want in our lives.

PRACTICE: **LOOK UP**

No one has ever lived a positive, happy, fulfilled life while at the same time staring down into the muck and wallowing in their negative thoughts. This is one reason why the cathedrals of old were built with high, arching ceilings—it invited people to look upward and assumed that posture tends to have a positive effect on our thinking. Try it out for yourself. The next time you catch yourself feeling depressed or simply bummed out, pay attention to your posture. As it turns out, the saying "Keep your chin up" isn't just an empty suggestion. Aligning your spine and lifting your gaze is often the first step to steering your thoughts in a preferable direction.

Some people think that the opposite of faith is disbelief, but I believe that the real opposite of faith is fear. When you have faith in something or someone, you feed energy in the direction of all the things you want out of life, helping those things manifest in the physical realm. When you are trapped in fear, however, all of your energy focuses on the things you don't want out of life. You fixate on the things you hope won't happen and obsess over them, which tends to make things worse. So, faith and fear are just different means of directing and focusing our energy. With mindfulness, we can become more conscious of where our thoughts dwell and therefore make better choices rather than mindlessly reacting to the world out of fear.

SPIRITUAL BYPASSING

Many people who embark upon a spiritual path fall prey to something called *spiritual bypassing*. One insidious way that spiritual bypassing takes shape is when people begin to believe that some emotional states are inherently more spiritual than others, which causes them to suppress their experience of fear or just pretend it isn't there in the first place. Again, this isn't the type of response to fear I'm talking about—nothing good comes from suppressing emotional energy. It simply manifests in unconscious ways, often in the form of health problems such as heart conditions and cancer. Ignoring fear doesn't cause it to dwindle or cease to exist in the slightest. Meditate, watch what's going on in your mind, see it for what it is, and steer your thoughts as gently as possible in a more beneficial direction.

VIBRATION

One last thing before we get into the basic practices. You hear people talk about *vibration* a great deal in magick. For our purposes here, all it essentially means is that when we have a low vibratory rate, it can feel quite unpleasant, because the flow of divine energy into our aura is being restricted in some way. Your first clue that this is happening is that you'll feel bad emotionally—stressed out, anxious, angry, impatient, jealous, and so on. Again, this is where meditation comes in handy, because most of the time we're not even aware that we're feeling terrible, or why. And as I've mentioned elsewhere, countless studies indicate that negative emotional states can contribute to everything from weight gain to heart attacks. Nobody needs that—especially if you're trying to learn and practice high magick.

Keep in mind that our emotions aren't what cause low vibrational rates—they're simply signals the body sends to warn us that our frequency is dropping. Emotions are the result of our thinking. Anytime you find yourself feeling sadness, it's an indication that you're engaging in thoughts that carry the vibratory rate we equate with sadness. On the other hand, if you're happy or experiencing joy, then your thoughts have been centered on love in some way (for yourself, for others, for the divine, etc.), and the emotion of happiness is an indication that your thoughts are in alignment with things of a higher vibrational rate.

PRACTICE: **TAKE CARE OF YOUR ENVIRONMENT**

Our immediate surroundings influence our thoughts and moods both directly and indirectly. I like to collect beautiful objects—magickal implements and paintings, mostly—and have found that they enrich the way I feel. Filling your home with uplifting and sensual objects will tend to lift your spirits and increase your vibrational rate.

Anytime you find yourself feeling unpleasant emotions, you can train your mind to become aware of the thoughts that gave birth to them, so that you can alter them in order to experience something different. To keep track of your thoughts, all you have to do is pay attention to your feelings.

CHAPTER 6

ESSENTIAL RITUALS AND INTERMEDIATE MODIFICATIONS

Most of the material in this chapter is what I focused on in *High Magick*. It's also the basis for the advanced practices to follow. I want to once again emphasize that magick works in layers—you can't just skip over the foundational techniques and move directly into summoning dozens of angels to manifest your practical magick. In other words, if you haven't already grounded yourself in what I presented in *High Magick*, here's your chance to spend some time with the essential practices and rituals before going forward. I've also included a couple of new applications for some of those practices, as well as some intermediate rituals you'll need to become familiar with for some of the material presented in chapter 8.

THE PENTAGRAM

I always like to begin with a little background information about pentagrams. People in the West automatically have creepy associations with these five-pointed stars, conjuring up all sorts of nightmarish or Satanic Hollywood imagery that have nothing to do with this sacred symbol whatsoever. The pentagram wasn't thought of in this way until the 1960s. In fact, it was once used as a symbol of Christianity, the points on the star representing the five wounds of Jesus. Long before that, the Greek philosopher and magician Pythagoras taught that the pentagram represents the powers of the four elements (see chapter 1), unified and blessed by the power of spirit, which is represented by the fifth and topmost point of the star. That's why we always depict the pentagram pointing upward—it symbolizes how everything in nature comes together to serve the purpose of the divine mind.

HISTORY OF MAGICK: THE BLACK LANDS

The core of a magickal practice is a process of internal alchemy that traces its roots back to the ancient Middle East, beginning in Mesopotamia and eventually finding its way into Egypt—the region around the Nile that was once known as Kemet. One explanation of this name, often translated as "the black land," is that it described how rich and fertile the soil was. In time, the spiritual practices of that culture were referred to as the "black arts." The term *black magick* wouldn't take on diabolical connotations until much later, when the Catholic Church would spend centuries attempting to stamp out any form of spirituality it considered to be a rival, including misrepresenting the symbols of other forms of worship as malevolent in some way.

You'll be using pentagrams quite a bit in the practices to come, namely by drawing them in the air with your hand to either banish or invoke energy. Either way, you trace them in flaming blue light. In banishing, you're cleansing all the unwanted energy out of a place in order to perform magick without interference—you want your work to only contain the energy you invite into your temple. When invoking, you're pulling that energy into your space or using it to bless, charge, protect, and empower other objects, places, and people.

When drawing the pentagram, you never use your own energy. Instead, you employ the infinite energy that surrounds, permeates, and actually composes the world around you. The way to do this is with your breath, envisioning the entire earth filling up with energy in the form of white light when you inhale, and then—by using the first two fingers on your right hand, also known as the *sword mudra*—drawing a pentagram in brilliant blue light (like the color of a pilot light on the stove) as you exhale.

If you're drawing the pentagram in the air, you can use your own body as a template to ensure that you're drawing each star roughly the same size. For banishing, you start at the level of your left hip, draw the line of blue light in front of you, up to the level of your forehead (the top of the star), then down to your right hip, over to your left shoulder, across to your right shoulder, and then back down to where you began at your left hip. When you follow this pattern, you can draw the pentagram in one smooth, unbroken line.

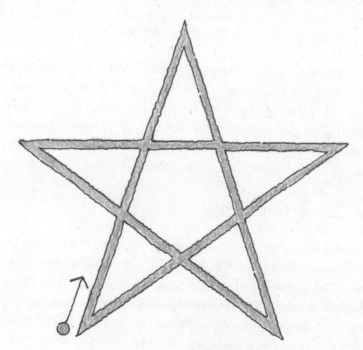

How to Draw a Banishing Pentagram

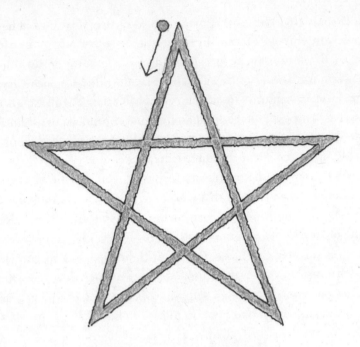

How to Draw an Invoking Pentagram

To draw the invoking pentagram, use the same body parts as your guide, but go in the opposite direction and begin at the top of the star; in other words, start at the level of your forehead, draw the line of flaming blue light down to your left hip, up to your right shoulder, and so on. By drawing the pentagram in this way, you're pulling the energy of the stars down from heaven and into the earth.

THE QABALISTIC CROSS

The Qabalistic Cross is the first (and often last) step to the Lesser Banishing Ritual of the Pentagram (LBRP), but it's also a great practice to do in its own right. In addition to keeping your aura balanced and stable, it helps clear out the gunk from your energetic body and prepare you for the powerful influx of divine light you're about to work with. It will also protect you from whatever negative energy you might encounter as you go about your day, keep you focused, and help diminish any anxieties you might be experiencing.

As far as symbols go, the cross also predates Christianity and is found in one form or another in cultures around the world. Magicians have used the cross for centuries to stand for complete balance of all aspects of our psyche. When we're in perfect balance, forces outside of us—human or otherwise—will have a much more difficult time implanting suggestions into our mind stream or otherwise influencing our energy field.

Keep in mind that the more you perform the Qabalistic Cross, the more vivid and powerful it will become. If you want your magick to progress, I recommend doing it at least twice a day, if not more. Only doing it once every six months or so is the equivalent of going to the gym once every six months—if that's your approach, don't be surprised if not much happens. On the other hand, if you make the Qabalistic Cross a part of your daily routine, the rate at which you'll progress will surprise you.

While performing the Qabalistic Cross, you'll be reciting a mantra that's essentially an ancient Hebrew version of part of the Lord's Prayer. Translated, the syllables mean "Thine in the kingdom, the power, and the glory forever." By vibrating this mantra in tandem with the visualization, you're informing the deeper parts of your psyche that the divine is already within you—in fact, you're reminding yourself that you've never been separated from the source of all creation. The Qabalistic Cross essentially works because it's designed to awaken the essence of God that lies dormant within you.

PRACTICE: **THE QABALISTIC CROSS**

1. Stand in the middle of the space you're using for this ritual and face east.

2. Close your eyes and imagine that your body is growing in size with every breath. With every inhalation, you grow

larger and larger, until eventually the earth is just a tiny dot beneath your feet and you are surrounded by the universe. Continue inhaling, and visualize your body growing even larger, until the entire universe is just a speck beneath your feet.

3. Focus on the center of your chest. Imagine that you see a glowing golden sphere there. If you recall the Tree of Life as presented in chapter 2, this sphere is the energy center that corresponds with Tiphareth.

4. Take slow, deep breaths, and imagine that this golden sphere of energy glows brighter and brighter with every breath you take. Eventually the energy grows to such an incredible amount that it explodes, shooting out through the top of your head in the form of a beam of white light. Imagine that the beam goes all the way to the very end of infinity and attaches there.

5. Using the sword mudra (the first two fingers of your right hand), touch your fingers to your forehead and vibrate the mantra *Ateh* (ah-tay).

6. Focus on the Tiphareth center once more, breathing into it and seeing it grow brighter and brighter with every in-breath you take. After three breaths, exhale and watch another beam of brilliant white light extend downward from Tiphareth through your lower torso, legs, and feet. Watch it travel downward to the very bottom of infinity and anchor itself there.

7. At this point, you are grounded above and below, such that nothing can buffet or move you.

8. Now move your fingers to the middle of your chest and vibrate the mantra *Malkuth* (mahl-kooth).

9. Focus again on the golden sphere in the middle of your chest and resume taking slow, even breaths. Watch as the sphere grows brighter until it eventually explodes, the beam of light shooting out through your right shoulder until it reaches the end of infinite space on that side of your body, connecting you there.

10. Now place the sword mudra of your right hand on your right shoulder. Vibrate *Vegeburah* (vey-geb-boo-rah) as your next mantra.

11. Bring your attention once more to the sphere in your chest. Inhale energy into it once more, watching as it grows more brightly. After three inhalations, exhale and envision the beam of white light extending from Tiphareth out through your left shoulder, all the way out to that side of infinity, anchoring you to that spot in a way that can never be broken.

12. Now touch your left shoulder with the sword mudra and vibrate *Vegehdula* (vey-ged-doo-lah).

13. One last time, focus on the golden sphere in your chest. Fold your hands over that spot and vibrate the mantra *Le Olam Amen* (lee oh-lam ah-men).

WE CONNECT HEAVEN AND EARTH

We were designed to be some sort of connection. We are connective tissues within some massively larger consciousness, and our function is to be a bridge from heaven to earth. We can strengthen our ability to do so, become more proficient at it. The energy of heaven is meant to flow through us and into the world, and we are connected to both through a fractal process in which a reflection of the macrocosm can be seen in the microcosm. I always knew this on a theoretical or intellectual level, but it was only through magick that I experienced it firsthand. What I'm describing here is essentially Christ, but it's also the Christ in every one of us when we awaken to our true nature.

THE LESSER BANISHING RITUAL OF THE PENTAGRAM

If you've been to any of my classes, you'll hear me talk about the LBRP over and over, perhaps to the point where you even become sick of hearing about it. I'm certain when I launch into another impassioned speech about how vital it is to do the LBRP daily, more than one of my students thinks, "Great—this again!" If you ever catch yourself feeling this way, please keep in mind that the LBRP has long been considered the Philosopher's Stone of ceremonial magick, and it was the only practice given initiates of the Hermetic Order of the Golden Dawn. They were expected to master it through and through, and only then would they be considered for the inner order.

All the advanced techniques in magick that lead to completion of the Great Work (spiritual immortality) are based on the LBRP—even those that involve overlapping pentagrams and hexagrams and the invocation of hundreds of angels and archangels. The LBRP protects your aura—kind of like wrapping your energetic body with divine insulation—and that makes it possible to invoke the type of energy it takes to boost your aura and ensure you don't suffer from unwanted dispersion of energy. It also empowers you to gradually begin to perceive the astral level of reality and harmonize the aspects of yourself that exist on that level (also known as Yesod on the Tree of Life). In short, all the emphasis I put on the LBRP is for a damn good reason!

LIGHT

When we do magick, we're almost always working with light. You'll hear talk in magickal circles of performing a particular exercise with light—for example, when drawing pentagrams or hexagrams. This light is not just something we visualize—it actually exists. It's what magicians of old called "astral light," and it's something we're actually directing when we visualize it. It's not light that comes from our own energy, which would quickly deplete us, but divine energy that we draw into ourselves.

RITUAL: THE LESSER BANISHING RITUAL OF THE PENTAGRAM

The outline given below will suit your purposes for the practices to follow. That being said, if you're interested in a more detailed and unpacked version of the LBRP (including the practice of adding Metatron and Sandalphon to the LBRP), see chapter 13 of *High Magick*.

1. Perform the Qabalistic Cross as instructed earlier.

2. Facing east, inhale deeply and visualize filling the entire earth beneath your feet with light.

3. With your right hand in the sword mudra, trace a banishing pentagram (following the instructions found earlier in this chapter) in the air in front of you.

4. Take another deep breath and see the earth fill with even more light. Place the extended fingers of your hand through the center of the pentagram and visualize it flaring even more brightly as light from the earth flows back up through your body and into the pentagram.

5. Seal this energy into the pentagram by vibrating the mantra *Yehowah* (yay-ho-wah). Watch as the pentagram grows incredibly bright—as bright as your imagination can handle.

6. Inhale and see the earth fill once more with light. With your sword mudra, draw a line of white light from the center of the first pentagram around to the south side of your sacred space.

7. Take another deep breath in, watch as the earth is infused with light again, and trace another banishing pentagram on the southern side of your space.

8. As you inhale, the earth fills up with more light. Now place your sword mudra into the southern pentagram and watch it flare incredibly brightly. Vibrate the mantra *Adonai* (ah-don-eye).

9. Inhale once more and see the earth filling up with light beneath your feet. From the center of the southern pentagram, extend the line of white light you drew earlier around to the western side of your sacred space.

10. Take another deep breath and watch once more as the earth fills up with light. Trace another banishing pentagram in the west in front of you.

11. Inhale, watch as the earth fills up with light again, and place your sword mudra into the center of your western

pentagram. See the symbol intensify as brightly as you can make it and vibrate the mantra *Eheieh* (eh-hee-yay).

12. Inhale again and visualize that the earth glows greater and greater with bright light. Extend the line of white light now from the western pentagram to the north with the sword mudra.

13. Inhale, see the earth fill up with light, and trace another banishing pentagram in front of you on the north side of your sacred space.

14. Watch the earth once more become infused with light as you inhale. Thrust the sword mudra into the northern pentagram and imagine it flaring as brightly as you can. Vibrate the mantra *Agelah* (ah-gay-lah).

15. Inhale and see the earth fill up with light again. With the sword mudra, complete the circle of white light by tracing from the center of the most recent pentagram back around to the eastern side of your temple. Now there are four pentagrams of flaming blue light burning all around you, and they're all connected by this ring of white light.

16. Now you should be facing east again. Although more advanced practices will employ the LBRP as outlined here to work with various other angels and archangels, we'll start by envisioning the elemental archangels as described in chapter 1.

17. To begin, inhale and envision Archangel Raphael expanding from the eastern pentagram until his glowing form towers above you. Now say, "Before me, Raphael."

18. Breath in and visualize now that Archangel Gabriel grows from the center of the western pentagram behind you until she is bright and extremely large. Say, "Behind me, Gabriel."

19. Inhale and envision that Archangel Michael expands from the center of the southern pentagram. Now say, "On my right hand, Michael."

20. Finally, out of the pentagram on your left, imagine Archangel Uriel growing powerfully large to the north. Say, "On my left hand, Uriel."

21. Now see all four pentagrams burning even brighter than before. Say, "For about me flame the pentagrams."

22. Inhale and see a hexagram—a six-pointed star made of two interlocking triangles—in the center of your chest. Visualize the triangle pointing upward as red and the one pointing down as blue. Say, "Within me shines the six-rayed star."

23. See the circle of white light you've drawn through the middle of the pentagrams. Inhale again and watch as the circle expands upward, closing in on itself above you like the roof of a dome.

24. Inhale again and see the circle of light extend and close below you like the bottom of a dome. Now you're in the middle of a sphere made of white light. No negative energy can penetrate it.

25. As your closing step, perform the Qabalistic Cross once more.

INTERMEDIATE MODIFICATIONS TO THE LBRP

The Lesser Invoking Ritual of the Pentagram

The LBRP is all about purification and eliminating unwanted energies, but a slight modification to the practice turns it into an invoking ritual that calls upon higher forms of energies in the form of angels and archangels. The Lesser Invoking Ritual of the Pentagram entails pulling their divine energy into your sacred space and aura in a highly concentrated, yet balanced form. Envisioning yourself surrounded by these entities and being bathed in their protection and blessings has subtle yet noticeable effects on your consciousness, namely because the practice empowers you to experience the phenomenal world as your higher self as opposed to the way the ego sees it (or wants you to experience it).

If you've cleansed your temple and energetic body thoroughly with the LBRP before doing this practice, invoking angels and archangels will also foster the following effects. You will:

- Experience the present moment more thoroughly and with less conscious effort
- Increase the health and vitality of your energetic body
- Sharpen your mental focus
- Boost your physical stamina
- Drastically decrease stress and anxiety

The most basic form of the invocation practice resembles the LBRP in almost every way. The primary difference is that you use the invoking pentagrams I described earlier in this chapter. You can pull in divine energy in any number of ways, but the form I typically suggest beginning with is a simple energetic balancing that involves the four elements as embodied by the appropriate archangels (that is, the ones you employed in the LBRP). That being said, if one of the archangels or elements appeals to you or you have a more specific need in mind, feel free to use just one of them in each direction. For example, if there's a particular emotional trauma that you just can't shake, and you'd like some help healing that particular wound, I recommend invoking Gabriel in all directions—that is, not just in the west—and infusing yourself with a more powerful dose of her divine energy.

Some magicians are adamant about concluding any practice session with the LBRP in order to balance out any stray energies that might be left behind after a given ritual. Feel free to do that after your invoking practice, but I don't think it's much of an issue whenever you're invoking angels and archangels. In my experience, all the excess energy will either go into whatever practical magick you're doing or you'll absorb it directly into your aura.

Circumambulation

Again, this isn't a separate practice from the LBRP—it's just an intensifying modification to the invoking form of the ritual. Circumambulation is the conscious act of circling or walking around something, often for religious or spiritual reasons—Buddhists circumambulate holy sites, such as stupas; Muslims circumambulate the Kaaba; and modern-day wiccans circumambulate in their Cone of Power practice.

Here's how to add circumambulation to your practice: After you open your temple with all the appropriate pentagrams (and/or hexagrams—see chapter 8), walk in a clockwise direction around your sacred space. Each time you pass the eastern wall, stop for a moment and take a deep, powerful in-breath. Then, when you exhale, step forward and hurl the accumulated energy ahead of you. If you do this repeatedly while walking in a circle, it creates a spiral pattern that the energy will continue to follow. In fact, you can visualize the energy as an upside-down tornado of golden light that shines brighter and spins faster every time you pass the eastern quarter of your circle.

When you begin adding this modification, just do it three times. After you get used to that, try more, increasing the force with every repetition. When I was on death row, I'd circumambulate three hundred times, but, then again, I had a lot of time on my hands. The process would take hours, but it allowed me to build up massive amounts of energy, which I could then put into a visualization, talisman, blessed glass of water, or just ingest directly into my own aura.

When I did this daily, I'd use a different intention each week—one week it might be "May the light protect, guide, and illuminate me"; other times it would be something like, "Please protect my loved ones from harm" or "May I be home, free from prison." Most often, however, I'd just ingest the energy and silently wish to complete the Great Work in one lifetime.

Adding Elemental Angels, Rulers, and Kings

This is a modification I created while experimenting with the LBRP in prison. This version of the ritual is a fairly straightforward way to magnify its benefits, and I find it takes just a little bit longer to complete. Regardless, I don't recommend rushing through any of these practices. It's far more important to feel these energies and visualize them as clearly as possible (as well as the pentagrams of light) than it is to reach the end of the ritual.

The visualizations of the elemental angels, rulers, and kings are simply less powerful versions of the archangels you're already accustomed to envisioning. For example, the angels associated with the fire element are just less detailed versions of Archangel Michael, and the rulers and kings are the same. I simply visualize them standing in rows—archangels, angels, rulers, and then kings—almost as if there are four walls of these intelligences surrounding me in their corresponding colors.

To this version of the LBRP I also add the two archangels Metatron and Sandalphon (this is the same version of the ritual I outlined in *High Magick*). I see Metatron and the three angels of the *Qaioth Ha-Qodesh* (angels of the angelic choir) above me in brilliant white light, and Sandalphon and the three angels of the Ashim beneath my feet in bright beige. As above, I visualize the secondary intelligences as less powerful versions of their associated archangel.

Once you complete this practice, you should feel as if you're encased in a sphere of angelic energy. You might even be able to sense a tangible intelligence present there with you after you've practiced this ritual for a while.

Adding the Archangels of the Tree of Life

This is one of my favorite modifications to the LBRP, and—like the one just above—it will give you a taste of some of the advanced practices in chapter 8. All you have to do is, before closing, add the eight archangels of the Tree of Life in a ring outside of the elemental archangels. In the end, you should be standing in the center of two rings of archangels. This version of the LBRP always leaves me feeling as if I'm wearing a suit of armor made of pure angelic energy. It's an ideal practice for spiritual sustenance—you end up absorbing an incredible amount of ambient energy in the process.

When I was in prison, I also added energies of the Tree of Life to my invocation practice, although I primarily used the archangels and angels of Tiphareth, which is correlated with victory in all forms. And since Tiphareth is the sphere in the very center of the tree, it represents energies from both sides in a balanced and harmonious way.

The primary modification here is to vibrate *YHVH Eloah Va Da'ath* (yay-ho-wah el-oh-ah va da-aath) for the pentagrams instead of the usual mantras. This is the divine name associated with Tiphareth. Once you have the four pentagrams around you blazing and charged, begin invoking Raphael (the archangel of the sphere of Tiphareth) and Michael (the archangel of the planetary energy of Tiphareth—that is, the sun). Then invoke as many energies from the Malachim, the angelic choir associated with Tiphareth, as you can:

Before me, Raphael (see him towering
above you in brilliant gold robes)

Behind me, Michael (same visualization)

On my right hand, Malachim

On my left hand, Malachim

Above me, Malachim

Below me, Malachim

I would sometimes call up dozens of the Malachim—even hundreds—seeing them grow brighter as I vibrated their name. How many times you do this depends entirely upon how much energy you want to put into the ritual—if you're trying to manifest something relatively small, you only need to use a few. If it's something bigger, however (for example, in my case, not being executed and getting out of prison), you'll want to put as much energy as possible into it. Once you're satisfied or simply too exhausted to continue, visualize all of the pentagrams, archangels, and angels all around you turn into pure, golden light and saturate the image of your desired manifestation. Then release that vision to go wherever it needs to go in order to fulfill its task.

You can also visualize the accumulated energy going into a candle or talisman. If the former, just situate the unlit candle in the center of your space, see all the energy go into it in the form of brilliant light, and conclude by saying, "So mote it be" (or "Amen," if you're comfortable with it). Then light the candle for a given time, burn it for a certain amount each day, or allow it to go down all in one sitting. If doing this ritual with a talisman, carry it with you until whatever you want to manifest comes to pass.

I can personally vouch for the power of this particular ritual. Within a year of doing it every day for an hour or so, I walked out of prison and went home.

RITUAL: **THE ANALYSIS OF THE KEYWORD (OR LVX)**

Once you've cleared all the negative energy out of your sacred space by performing the LBRP, another way to consecrate your temple with an influx of divine light is by adding a short practice known traditionally as the Analysis of the Keyword Ritual, but which I prefer to call the LVX Ritual. In Latin, LVX means "light," and in this context we pronounce these three letters together as we would the plural of the name Luke. This particular modification to the LBRP also adds physical movement in such a way that we actually form the shape of these letters with our body. The combination of these gestures with our breathing and visualization calls into our space an incredibly powerful force of divine light that can also be channeled into objects (see the section on talismans in chapter 7) or other people in need, regardless of their proximity to us.

1. Begin by standing at the center of the space where you have performed the LBRP. Close your eyes and bring your attention at the very top of the universe, where you see a brilliant white light shining. Know that this light represents the source from which everything came and to which everything will one day return.

2. As you remain focused on the divine light above you, begin to take slow, deep breaths, seeing that light above you grow brighter with every inhalation.

3. Slowly raise your right arm until it is held high above your head, while your left arm is pointed out to the side. Say "El" out loud, seeing the light above you flare even more powerfully.

4. Next, raise both hands above your head so that you are forming the shape of a V. See the light above you shine even brighter as you say "Vee."

5. Lower both arms and cross your hands over your chest. As you say "Ex," the light at the top of the universe should glow blindingly bright.

6. In a voice of authority, say, "Let the divine light descend." See a blast of white light come from the source above you down through the universe to fill up the room or space where you are standing. It should saturate

the entire area from floor to ceiling with white light, including your own body.

7. Hold the image of your space filled with light in your mind's eye. See it glowing more brilliantly every time you inhale. As you vibrate the divine mantra *IAO* (ee-ah-oh), see all of the light in the room grow as powerful as possible.

8. Either conclude here by performing the Qabalistic Cross or continue on with any other mindfulness or magick practices you wish to do.

ABBREVIATED FORM OF THE LVX RITUAL

When I was in prison, I had very little privacy and knew for certain that I was regularly being watched. For this reason, I developed an abbreviated form of the ritual described above so that I could complete it privately in an unobtrusive, unnoticeable way, because I didn't want to trigger the guards by doing something they'd consider evil or weird. In my experience, that typically resulted in them inflicting more pain on me. Basically, I did the LVX Ritual without any outward movement at all, lying on my bunk with my eyes closed, doing my best to relax my body and visualize everything in the practice. I also experimented with the mantras and colors manifested by the divine light—using golden light (representing Tiphareth) to send healing energy to a sick friend, and vibrating Raphael's name or red (the sphere of Geburah) and the mantra Kamael to surround myself with protective energy. Out of prison, I've also used Archangel Tzadkiel and the color blue for prosperity or black light and Tzaphkiel's name in order to not be noticed in public. (Fair warning: it doesn't actually make you invisible; it just sort of camouflages your appearance so that you blend into the background.)

CHAPTER 7

CALLING ON ANGELS

Before we get into the advanced practices of ceremonial magick presented in the next chapter, I want to offer some straightforward practices (mostly oriented toward manifestation) that build on the work you've already done and give you a few more ways of employing the Lesser Banishing Ritual of the Pentagram (LBRP). Some people mistakenly believe that magick necessarily involves lengthy, archaic, and overly complex rituals. Granted, some practices can be accurately described that way, but most of the ones included in this chapter are deceptively simple. That being said, the more you engage in the fundamental practices of magick, such as the Qabalistic Cross and the LBRP, the better the outcome will be in all the other magick you do, regardless of its complexity.

When working with angels and archangels, I've come to realize that they don't carry out the tasks we charge them with just because we ask them to—they do it because they perceive the divine within us. The more we can purify and cleanse our energetic bodies, the more these intelligences receive our prayers and requests as if they come from the source of creation itself. Devoting ourselves to mindfulness and energy work actually helps the angels and archangels see beyond our small, limited, and egoic sense of self and thereby encourages their assistance.

In the end, all the practices included in this book come down to one thing—energy. The more time and effort you dedicate to what you're doing, the more energy you put into it. Some people will also find they have better results with one practice than another, which is why I've included so many here. I'll start with some of the simpler ones and then move on from there.

PRACTICE: **MODERN-DAY BIBLIOMANCY**

Let's start with a practice that people have been doing for thousands of years, mostly with holy books (namely, the Bible and the Quran), but also with revered works of literature (in particular, the epics of Homer and Virgil). Whenever they felt like they needed some divine guidance or a higher form of advice, they'd flip open the chosen text at random, place their finger down without looking, and glean some meaning from whatever word or passage their finger found. If you resonate with the texts mentioned above (or any others, for that matter), feel free to adopt the following practice for them, but this modern take on bibliomancy employs the great unfolding text that most of us use all the time: the internet.

1. Consider the issue or topic you want assistance with.

2. Invoke an angel or archangel you either feel connected to or whom you think is appropriate to this particular issue.

3. Initiate a web search either by using keywords or employing a random content service.

4. See what comes up. Try not to offhandedly dismiss the results. I've found that what arises when I employ this practice sometimes won't make sense for days or weeks.

RITUAL: **SIMPLE BLESSING RITUAL**

I talked about vibratory rates earlier in the book. One great way to bring your own vibration up as high as possible is through blessing rituals—for yourself, for other people, and for objects. In magick, this is also known as *consecration*, because through these blessings we consecrate something for a specific purpose— ideally for divine service. You can do the following practice at any time, but it's also helpful to add it before doing any form of magick you might already be performing. If you're working with others who are physically present, I recommend blessing them and then asking them to return the favor by blessing you. Even if you just use this practice to bless another person, you still receive a lot of benefit yourself, because it's another way to get better at increasing your vibratory rate, harnessing energy, and moving that energy around in a more conscious, mindful way.

1. Inhale and visualize the earth below you filling up with white light.

2. As you say "Blessed be your mind, so that it is open and receptive to truth," draw a cross made of white light on the person's forehead (or your forehead, in the event that you're blessing yourself). This cross isn't like the one used in Christianity—the crossing, perpendicular lines are the same length (a perimeter around the four terminal points would create a square, as opposed to a rectangle).

3. See the light rushing back up from the earth, into your body, out through your hand, and into the cross of light as you draw it.

4. Inhale, see the earth fill up with white light again, and say, "Blessed be your heart, so that it is open to the giving and receiving of love" while seeing the light move up from the

earth, through your body, and into the cross as you draw it over the person's heart.

5. Breathe in, imagine that the earth once more is infused with white light, and say, "Blessed be your hands, that they may be strong enough to do the work that will be required of them" while repeating the process described above.

6. Finally, bless the person's feet in a similar manner by saying, "Blessed be your feet, so that they may carry you to the completion of your journey."

For more on blessings like this one, particularly on how to involve angels and archangels in them, I highly recommend Silver RavenWolf's *Angels: Companions in Magick* that I mentioned in chapter 3, in which she offers various ways to bless and consecrate your altar, magickal implements, body, and so on. I've learned a great deal from her work over the years, and I still rely on her expertise to this day. In particular, the book mentioned above helped me understand a number of complicated procedures I never could figure out in more serious tomes devoted to magick.

PRACTICE: **BARE-BONES MANIFESTATION**

Both our brain and our heart emit electromagnetic fields that constantly interact with the quantum field in which we exist. As it turns out, the field generated by the heart is much larger than the one generated by the brain, but both serve an important purpose. For example, holding an image in our mind imprints that image on the quantum field. The heart also visualizes, but employs feelings instead. This means that if we hold an image of ourselves that indicates a positive feeling state—for example, smiling with happiness because we were recognized for doing a good job at work—we actually help the heart and mind work together to manifest positive results on the physical plane. (See Rick Hanson's "Take in the Good" practice as a great take on this.[1])

This directly pertains to angels and archangels if you consider that a number of magicians throughout the centuries have taught that the very field in which we exist is itself composed of angelic energy. This means that we are constantly in communication with these intelligences whether we know it or not. If that's the case, I think it's a much better idea to be doing so with great skill and clear intent.

You can use this practice for anything, really, but in the following outline I'm using the example of better physical health, simply because most of us can usually benefit from something like that. When I was in prison, it was a constant desire of mine to be pain-free and healed from the psychological and physical trauma inflicted upon me, and I'm sure that at some point in your life this practice will come in handy.

1. Think about whatever is ailing you, whether it be chronic pain, heartache, or even the discomfort that comes from a bad rash. Now, instead of focusing on your particular suffering, imagine what it would be like to be completely free of it. Hold a clear picture of yourself in that state in your mind. Are you smiling? Is your body at ease and relaxed? Are you simply able to walk around and actually pay attention to your surroundings? Really explore what it would actually look like to be completely free of your ailment.

2. Now try to really *feel* the sense of relief and joy that would come if you were completely healthy.

3. Hold that visualization and feeling for as long as you can. Try for a couple of minutes. If you get distracted,

remember the meditation instructions from chapter 5—simply come back to the image as clearly as you can.

4. When you've done this practice for a couple of minutes, offer a sincere moment of gratitude to the angels and archangels. Thank them for working on the issue and know that they're already on the job.

Feel free to do this practice as often as you'd like. Keep in mind, too, that it's best to not keep track of the results of your practical magick on the physical realm. That being said, if you do this practice thoroughly, it shouldn't take long to see results.

PRACTICE: **SHIELDING**

Here's another simple ritual. It employs more of the skills you developed with the LBRP, as well as the relationship you fostered therein with Archangel Michael.

As I've said elsewhere, energy is contagious. We're exchanging energy constantly with other people, the objects we touch, and the places we visit. Unfortunately, not all those exchanges are pleasant or beneficial. When I was in prison, for example, I was surrounded by overlapping fields of terribly negative energy. Death row is a hellish place in and of itself, and there are people there guilty of some of the most hair-raising and heinous acts imaginable, not to mention mental illness on an institutional level. For this reason, I developed this quick shielding technique from some of the more complicated banishing rituals, because you don't always have time to enact a proper ritual in prison. Here's the basic gist of it.

1. Stand quietly with your eyes closed. Begin inhaling, and as you inhale, see yourself as inhaling chi or some form of powerful light.

2. As you inhale this energy, watch as it travels through your body and out through your feet into the earth beneath you, completely filling it with white light. With each inhalation, the earth beneath your feet grows brighter and brighter, filled with more and more of this divine energy.

3. After anywhere from three to ten breaths (depending on how strong you want your shield to be, or how long you want it to last), point your right arm out in front of you at about waist high or slightly higher, holding your hand in the sword mudra.

4. Picture all the energy within the earth rushing back up through your body and out through your hand as you slowly turn in place, drawing a circle of white light around yourself with your extended fingers.

5. Once you've gone all the way around in a circle, see the energy surround you in a ring, almost like a hula hoop made entirely of white light.

6. Now reach out with both hands at your sides, palms up. Slowly raise your arms and bring your palms together above your head, almost as if doing a slow-motion jumping jack. As you perform this movement, envision that you are stretching the circle of light upward until it eventually closes above your head like a dome.

7. Now do the same thing with palms facing down, stretching the circle of light until it closes beneath your feet like a dome.

8. When you're finished, you should see yourself as being enclosed in a spherical or egg-shaped protective bubble of light.

9. Take a moment to inhale and see the sphere glow as brightly as you can possibly visualize. Say to yourself, "May the protective light of the angels surround and shield me from all external energies. I ask this in the divine name of Michael."

Since you can invoke for protection a number of the angels and archangels cataloged in part 1 of this book, feel free to modify this practice accordingly.

PRACTICE: SHORT PLANETARY INVOCATION

Here's another quick way to invoke the energies of archangels through the planetary lens I mentioned in chapters 2 and 3. You can do the following visualization in a couple of different ways. Here's the first:

1. Sit quietly for a couple of minutes and let your thoughts settle.

2. When your mind has cleared somewhat, envision the planet you wish to invoke, visualizing it situated far above you in space.

3. Inhale and see the image of that planet grow brighter and brighter with its associated color—for example, you could visualize Mercury as an orange sphere of light.

4. After doing step 3 several times, exhale and see a burst of colored energy come from that particular planet, descending through space and entering your aura with tremendous force.

Another way to do this practice is to visualize the planetary archangels themselves, wearing robes of that planet's colors. In this version, the burst of energy comes from your visualization of the archangel.

Regardless of which way you choose to do this practice, try to bring as much intensity and sharpness to the visualization as possible. Repeat the process three times. You can also do either form of this invocation by directing the energy not into your own aura but into someone else's or an external object of some sort (a candle, crystal, piece of jewelry, or—as we're just about to get into next—a talisman).

When you're done, release any visualizations from your mind and go about your day. Just know that the planetary energy and archangelic intelligence you invoked are there, continuing to saturate you with their energy and power even when you're not thinking about them.

HISTORY OF MAGICK: SECRECY AND SILENCE

Since the time of ancient Sumer, there have been two ways of understanding mythology: in short, front speech and back speech. Front speech was exoteric—it was intended for the masses, and from this presentation evolved most of the religious forms we know of today. Back speech was esoteric—it was meant only for initiates who were taught how to understand the information encoded within symbolism. Magick is primarily back speech. For various reasons, magicians typically do not describe higher-level experiences to adherents before their consciousnesses are primed for reception, instead giving students techniques that will enable them to experience realizations themselves. Ideally, these techniques are not hidden in secret as much as they are withheld until the student is ready to benefit from them. The long tradition of maintaining silence in magick isn't just about secrecy; it's also about protecting others from misunderstanding and oneself from the machinations of the ego. We cultivate internal silence by practicing it externally—otherwise our personal gnosis and experiences become subject to decay. When secrecy actually comes into play in magick, it's because people were under constant threat from the Catholic Church, they wanted to hoard magick and its power for themselves, or there were practices that were actually dangerous to initiate (or, in some cases, fatal) without the requisite purifications. When the Buddha famously refused to answer profound questions about the origins and nature of the universe, he didn't say that he didn't know—he simply ignored the question. This was a matter of an extremely powerful magician protecting his students. The Buddha said that to ask such questions—for example, "How did samsara, the endless wheel of suffering, begin?"—is to be like a person who has been shot with an arrow. Instead of going straight to a healer, the person demands to know what type of wood the arrow is made of, what style of bow fired the arrow, how tall the person was who used the bow, and so on. When you're actively dying, all this information is entirely beside the point.

PRACTICE: TALISMANS AND SIGILS

You can turn just about anything into a talisman. Some people get great results from putting angelic energy into candles, for example, so they use candles as much as possible in their rituals and in their lives, typically choosing colors that correspond with given angels or archangels, or maybe just using a white candle (since white contains the entire color spectrum). Other people prefer to craft talismans themselves or use more natural materials, such as wood, stone, and crystal. Whatever speaks to you and seems to work, I recommend choosing a color that aligns with the angelic energy you wish to invoke (for example, a red stone for protection—red being the color of the sphere of Geburah, where the seraphim reside). That being said, you can even make a type of talisman out of immaterial objects such as visualizations, which is actually my preferred method.

Due to their simplicity and power, I also like to use sigils. Anyone who spends more than a few minutes researching magick online will eventually come across sigils—designs that look like squiggly lines that embody abstract concepts or represent the names of divine energies (in this case, a sigil is essentially a chant of that energy's name in physical form). In this day and age, you'd be surprised at how many old books on magick have been uploaded to the internet, and a number of them include traditional sigils that have been used by magicians for centuries and are therefore imbued with the energy of all the people who have worked with them. For example, try a search for *Archangel Michael sigil* and see how many results pop up. You can also find the original grimoires in which given sigils first publicly appeared (one of the best known being the *Grimoire of Armadel*), even if the artists or authors of those books are now unknown. Any of these images can be downloaded or copied for your use.

You can also design sigils yourself. I actually prefer this method—drawing all my own sigils when I create a talisman. One simple method for doing so involves removing all the repeating letters from a name and combining what remains into shapes. There aren't any hard-and-fast rules to the process—you can add and remove as you see fit, eventually landing on what appears to be a completely meaningless doodle that somehow seems right to you, and that's what you use for your sigil.

The traditional method I use involves drawing a rose and placing a Hebrew letter on each petal, then translating those letters into their English-language counterparts. To make a sigil, you just place a transparent piece of paper over the rose and draw lines connecting the letters that spell out the angel or archangel's name. For example, for Anael, you would begin at the petal with an *A* on it, and then draw a line connecting it to the letter *N*, and so on. If you're interested in learning more about these methods or others, I suggest *Modern Magick: Twelve Lessons in the High Magickal Arts* by Donald Michael Kraig and *Angelic Sigils, Keys, and Calls: 142 Ways to Make Instant Contact with Angels and Archangels* by Ben Woodcroft. The sigils I have created for the elemental and zodiacal archangels are included in this book for your use.

Regardless of where you get the sigil from, when you employ an angelic or archangelic sigil to create a talisman, it invokes that particular intelligence to grant its power and blessing to the given object. The talisman you construct with the sigil is a direct line of connection to the angel or archangel, and it can be employed to communicate with them, in addition to having the power to invest other objects with the particular power of that angel or archangel.

RITUAL: **BASIC SIGIL PRACTICE**

To invoke any angel or archangel included in this book, simply photocopy the talisman and place it on your shrine, or draw the sigil yourself (that is, the squiggly line in the center of the talisman) in red ink on an object or person. You don't have to draw it in ink or paint (although you can, if you prefer)—the important thing is to draw it in light with the energy you pull in through the breathing and visualization practices already described.

1. Start this practice by performing the LBRP.

2. At this point, some people like to light a candle in honor of their Holy Guardian Angel (HGA; the specific voice in which God gives personal instruction), requesting its assistance and protection. This is optional, of

course, especially if you haven't established much of a relationship with your HGA yet.

3. Next, begin taking slow, deep breaths. With every inhalation, envision yourself drawing energy in from the universe around you. It passes through your body and into the earth in the form of light. See the entire earth beneath your feet fill with light. With each breath, the light grows more and more powerful.

4. Using your right hand as the sword mudra, trace the sigil of the archangel before you. See it being drawn in the light that accumulated in the earth beneath your feet, which rushes back up through your body and into the sigil. Even if you can't see it, or if you feel as if your powers of visualization are less than perfect, just know that you are drawing the sigil in light.

5. Call upon the archangel and state your desire. This can be done as simply as saying something like, "Archangel so-and-so, please hear me and heed my call. Come quickly to me and fulfill my desire without delay. I call upon you to go forth and fulfill my will to such and such a goal." Of course, instead of saying "so-and-so" and "such-and-such," state the angel or archangel's name (e.g., Michael or Amnitziel) and your specific desire (e.g., to be able to afford a new car in order to get to work and back more efficiently).

6. End the ritual by thanking the invoked intelligence, as if the result wasn't pending but rather already fulfilled.

You might not see any apparent signs, but angels and archangels begin to act behind the scenes the moment they are called upon. For example, in the Bible, Daniel calls upon an angel for help but then doesn't see a result until much later. The angel tells him that it started working right away, but that en route it had to overcome many obstacles. Remember this story if you don't notice immediate results, and keep in mind that the energies are without question already acting on your behalf.

PRACTICE: **THE GATEWAY TALISMAN**

Using traditional methods, I designed and charged the sigil pictured below (what I call the Gateway Talisman) specifically to help facilitate and enhance contact with the archangels of the Tree of Life. The following practice only takes a few moments to complete, and it only has to be done once.

The Gateway Talisman

1. Spend a couple of minutes relaxing as best you can. Let all the tension drain from your body and let go of whatever worries are bothering you for just a few minutes.

2. Let your eyes trace around the talisman. You don't have to be able to read it or understand what it means; this would be counterproductive, because we want the image to bypass your conscious mind and sink into the deeper realms of your psyche.

3. First follow the characters that are inside the double rings. Just follow them with your eyes, clockwise around the circle. As you trace the shape of the characters with your eyes, see yourself tracing over them with golden light. You don't have to see this clearly—what's important is your intent. If it helps with the visualization process, you can even trace the characters with your finger, pouring light into them the way you do when drawing the pentagrams during the LBRP.

4. Now do the same thing with the sigil in the center of the talisman. Begin with the small circle and end with the bar. See it in glowing golden light as you trace it with your eyes or finger.

5. Now focus on the golden energy center in the middle of your chest. This represents Tiphareth, the seat of our consciousness. Close your eyes and envision the talisman inside the golden sphere where your heart is located.

6. Take three deep breaths. As you inhale, see the talisman glow brighter and brighter within you, and as you exhale, see it grow even brighter still.

7. Lastly, open your eyes and look at the talisman. Trace it one final time with your eyes or finger, drawing the characters in light.

Don't worry about whether you did this practice long enough, whether you did it right, or anything else like that. Remember that an intention to connect with the angels is the most important part of the process. Once you've done this practice, you and I have successfully done magick together, whether you feel any different or not. And whenever you offer a sincere invitation to the archangels to work with you, they will always respond.

PRACTICE: **AIR MAGICK**

In the introduction to this book, I tell the story of how I invoked angels and archangels to create *High Magick*. Specifically, before I'd go into the studio at Sounds True, I'd close my eyes and invoke Raphael over and over again. I can't remember what I said exactly—something like, "Raphael, archangel of the intellect, help me speak my truth in a way that people will understand and be moved by"—but it worked. During the

The Sigil of Raphael, the Archangel of Air

recording, the magick poured out of me like a flood, and I was suddenly able to practice magick in a way I hadn't been able to since I was on death row.

The previous image is the traditional sigil for Raphael, which some of the most powerful magicians have used for centuries. Every single time someone uses this sigil, the energetic connection to Raphael becomes even stronger, and the following practice uses it to work powerful *air magick*.

1. Stand in front of a mirror, ideally somewhere you won't be disturbed for a few minutes (even if it means locking yourself in the bathroom).

2. Focus on your reflection and begin inhaling while envisioning that with every breath, you are filling the earth beneath your feet with light. Three to five breaths should be enough.

3. See Archangel Raphael standing behind you. Say, "Raphael, archangel of the east and ruler of the element of air, may your power, your blessing, and your favor descend upon me so that [*state your particular desire here*]."

4. Using your right hand as the sword mudra, draw the sigil of Raphael over your reflection in the mirror. It should be made of the same flaming blue light you use to draw the pentagrams in the LBRP.

5. Inhale and see the sigil glow as brightly as possible over your reflection. Vibrate Raphael's name.

As instructed elsewhere, go about your day knowing that your magick has already worked and your request has already been granted. Remember to not hold too tightly to what results are supposed to look like, but feel free to repeat the above practice once a day for a week or so.

PRACTICE: **FIRE MAGICK**

When I was in prison, Archangel Michael was my constant companion. Part of my daily rituals involved calling on him to stand guard in front of my cell door and protect me from vindictive guards. If you know what I look like, you'll recall that there are sigils, cyphers, and talismans of all sorts tattooed all over my body, and most of these designs have to do with archangels in one way or the other, but the very first one I had done after I got out of prison was in honor of Michael.

The Sigil of Michael, the Archangel of Fire

The possible reasons for invoking Michael in chapter 1 include protection, assistance in competition, and several other things, but I've also met with a lot of success asking for Michael's help regarding physical fitness and appearance. Whatever your reason for invoking this elemental archangel, start by obtaining a red candle. The size and shape of the candle isn't important; what matters is that you charge it with fire energy.

1. Place your candle on the altar or dedicated surface where you perform your magick.

2. Begin taking slow, deep breaths, envisioning that the entire earth beneath your feet is filling with white light with every inhalation.

3. Once you've held this visualization of the earth for a few moments, use all of that power to draw an invoking pentagram in the air right above the candle using the sword mudra.

4. Inhale into the earth once more, filling it up with light. Then thrust your fingers into the center of the pentagram and see it flare even more brightly. Vibrate Michael's name.

5. See the pentagram blaze as brightly as possible with the power of the name you have vibrated into it.

6. Now, using the tip of a nail or some other object suitable for carving, scratch Michael's sigil into the red candle. It doesn't have to be perfect—just copy the sigil as best you can.

7. Begin inhaling energy into the earth beneath your feet. Once you've built that image up as brightly as possible, use your fingers as the sword mudra to trace the sigil in light over the sigil now carved into the candle.

8. See the two versions of the sigil merge, becoming one and the same.

9. One last time, inhale light into the earth. Thrust your first two fingers down upon the sigil and see it glow even more brightly.

10. Now say something like, "I invoke Michael, archangel of fire and guardian of the south, to aid and assist me with the

goal of [*state your particular goal here, e.g., protection, losing weight, increasing passion in my life*]. May it come about in a way that is for the good of all and the harm of none."

11. Vibrate the mantra *Amen*, light the candle, and let it burn down completely.

If necessary, repeat this ritual once a month until you obtain sufficient results.

PRACTICE: **WATER MAGICK**

Remember when I said I didn't have access to magickal tools when I was in prison? That's not exactly true. Although I didn't have a proper chalice (the elemental tool associated with Gabriel), I was given a yellow plastic coffee cup, and I drank everything out of this cup while I was on death row. I also used it to ask Gabriel's blessings for emotional strength, stability, and happiness with the following practice (which, as you'll see, also involves the assistance of the other archangels of the elements).

I suggest using water, which is Gabriel's element. Water also has some interesting properties, including the ability to hold energy better than any other substance found on earth (with the possible exception of quartz crystal). The physical substance we know as water is not the same thing as the elemental energy of water—water on the material plane is such a pure container for energy that it can be charged with anything, including fire energy. Finally, water's also great to charge as a talisman, because after your ritual you can literally swallow the energy you've put into it. That water physically becomes a part of you, and the energy it contains alters the etheric plane as well.

Like the Earth Magick practice that follows, this is a talismanic ritual that involves objects—in this case, water and the cup or chalice of your choice—but doesn't require sigils.

1. Perform the Qabalistic Cross.

2. Perform the Lesser Invoking Ritual of the Pentagram as described in the previous chapter.

3. Take your chalice that holds water and move to the east of your temple. Say something like, "Raphael, archangel of the east, allow the power and blessings of the element of air to descend upon this water in order to protect and guide me."

4. Envision Raphael holding his caduceus above you and see a beam of brilliant yellow light come from it and shine down on the water you are holding.

5. Inhale three times, seeing the light that saturates the water grow a brighter and brighter yellow until the entire container glows brilliantly.

6. Now turn to face south. Say, "Michael, archangel of the south, allow the power and blessings of the element of fire to descend upon this water in order to protect and guide me."

7. Visualize Michael with his sword towering above you. Watch as a ray of bright red light issues from it and enters the water in your chalice.

8. Take three in-breaths. See the light from Michael's sword grow bright in the water until your chalice is illuminated intensely.

9. Now face the west and repeat the same invocation to Gabriel: "Gabriel, archangel of the west, allow the power and blessing of the element of water to descend upon this water in order to protect and guide me."

10. See Gabriel standing above you. A shaft of luminous blue light comes from the chalice she holds and enters your water.

11. Inhale three times and watch as the blue light saturates your water, which grows brighter and brighter until your entire container appears made of blue light.

12. Turning north in your temple, say, "Uriel, archangel of the north, allow the power and blessing of the element of earth to descend upon this water in order to protect and guide me."

13. Envision Uriel holding the pentacle towering above you. A beam of rich, green light issues from the pentacle and shines into the water you're holding.

14. Breathe in three times and watch as the light grows more intense until your chalice glows a brilliant green.

15. Now return to the middle of the circle and hold your chalice above your head, as if in offering to the heavens. Say, "May the power of spirit descend upon this chalice in order to protect, guide, and illuminate me."

16. See a beam of white light descend into your water, coming down from the source of all creation.

17. Inhale three times. See the water glow brighter and brighter. Now vibrate the word *Amen*.

18. Drink the water and see the white light completely fill your body—from the tips of your toes to the top of your head.

19. Do the Qabalistic Cross.

20. Perform the LBRP.

PRACTICE: **EARTH MAGICK**

A long time ago, magicians of old called pentacles (especially in their tarot context) "coins." Magicians eventually did away with that, because pentacles are about a lot more than just money—in fact, they represent the entire realm of magick itself. Uriel is considered the patron saint of magicians (especially when it comes to prosperity magick), and this explains why he's associated with the pentacles suit of the tarot.

Whether it be the tarot, tea reading, or any system of runes, one of Uriel's specialties is divination. Uriel's the archangel we go to for help in deciphering the deeper meaning of the messages we come across in this type of magick, so it's always a good idea to ask him to bless the tools of your choice and transform them into talismans of clear and accurate divination. This is one of the least complex practices you can do in this chapter, and it only takes a few minutes to complete.

1. Place your divination tool on your altar or a dedicated surface in front of you.

2. Inhale deeply and visualize Uriel expanding in front of you. With each in-breath, see him grow more solid and vibrant.

3. Now offer a heartfelt invocation. It doesn't need to be fancy or lengthy—just let your intention come through

as clearly as possible and don't worry too much about how you articulate it. I like to say something like, "Uriel, archangel of the earth and guardian of magicians, allow your power and blessings to descend upon these cards (because my divination tool of choice is the tarot) so that I may know things true and hidden. Help me express myself in a way that will be of the most use to my client and may all of this come about in a way that brings harm to none and is for the good of all."

4. See a shaft of green light descend from the heavens until it envelops your divination tool. Take several additional deep breaths and see your implement grow brighter and brighter.

5. After several moments of maintaining this visualization, know that your tool is blessed. Vibrate the mantra *Amen* in conclusion.

CHAPTER 8

ADVANCED RITUALS

Before we move on, I want to stress how important the preliminary practices found in chapters 5 and 6 are if you want these advanced rituals to work or simply make much sense to you. Just as you can't go from sitting on the couch for months and expect to finish a marathon the very next day, you must have some basic mastery of the LBRP before you engage in the complex techniques you'll find in this chapter. It's important that you don't feel rushed to get to the "good stuff" found here. When it comes to magick, the good stuff only comes from the quality of your intentions and practice, no matter what form of magick you're doing.

RITUAL: THE ROSE CROSS

I began doing this exercise daily while in prison, mostly to help cope with my ongoing physical pain (one of the beneficial side effects of this practice is pain relief). It should never be used in place of any of the basic pentagram rituals; it's best added after them to add power and blessing to any other magick you have performed.

Just as the LBRP equilibrates the aspects of us associated with the plane of Yesod, the Rose Cross ritual harmonizes the parts of us that exist higher on the Tree of Life, in the sphere of Tiphareth. This practice employs several techniques you're already accustomed to—inhaling and visualizing the earth filling up with light, for example. But one primary difference between this ritual and the LBRP is that the energetic boundary you draw around your temple here is shaped more like a cube (as opposed to a circle), according to the walls, floor, and ceiling of the room you find yourself in.

Most people find the Rose Cross ritual to be a lot more complicated and difficult to perform than the LBRP, at least at first. The frustration and confusion I felt the first few times I tried it were almost enough to make me quit, but there was just something compelling about it that made me keep trying, so much so that I became obsessed with it to the point of dreaming about it at night. One thing that really helped me get over the hump was having the instructions right there with me as I walked from corner to corner in the room.

As I've said elsewhere, the cross is a universally important symbol that predates Christianity by thousands of years. The cross used in this ritual represents the four cardinal directions, as well as the four elements that are transformed within us through the discipline of magick.

1. Stand in the closest approximation of the southeast corner of your room. As you inhale, see the earth fill up with light; as you exhale, draw a cross of golden light in the corner.

2. Inhale and once more visualize the earth expanding with divine light. This time, when you exhale, draw a circle of red light over the middle of the gold cross you created (much like the image of a Celtic cross).

3. Take another in-breath, watch the earth infuse with light, and place the first two fingers of your right hand into the center of your cross. Vibrate the mantra *Yeshua* (yay-hesh-yoo-ah).

4. Inhale and see the earth fill with light. This time, as you exhale, draw a line of white light from the center of the gold cross in the southeast corner of the room around to the southwest corner.

5. Repeat steps 1 through 4, drawing gold crosses with overlaid circles of red light and charging each of them with the divine name of Yeshua, connecting the four corners with a line of white light. When you complete the circuit, you should find yourself standing in a square of white light surrounded by encircled crosses in each of the four corners.

6. Now you'll add two more crosses—one above and one below—in order to seal your sacred space in all six directions. You do this precisely the same way as before—inhaling, filling the earth with light, exhaling, drawing the crosses as described, and charging them with the divine name—all while standing in the middle of the room.

7. Begin by drawing a line of white light from your original cross (that is, the one in the southeast corner of the room) to the ceiling. After drawing and charging the cross above you, visualize the line of white light connecting that cross to the one on the northwest corner of your space.

8. Inhale, fill the earth with light again, exhale, and continue the white line from the northwest cross down to the center of the room on the floor beneath you. Visualize and charge the cross there and then follow the same

directions to draw the line of white light back over to the southeast corner of your temple.

9. Take another in-breath, fill the earth with energy once more, and retrace the line that connects the southeastern cross with the one in the southwest. Then do the same to draw the line from the southwest up the wall and across to the cross on the ceiling.

10. Following the same procedure, continue to draw the line from the ceiling to the cross in the northeast corner, then to the cross in the center of the floor, then to the one in the southwest corner, then to the northwest, to the northeast, and finally to the original cross in the southeast of your sacred space. Each time you connect the corners, be sure to inhale, visualize the earth filling up with light, and exhale as you draw the line.

11. Take another deep in-breath, see the earth infused with energy, and place your sword mudra into the center of the southeastern circle and charge it once more with the divine name.

12. In the end, you should be standing in the center of the room in the middle of a visualized cube with gold and red crosses in all four corners, as well as above and below.

13. Conclude the Rose Cross ritual by performing the abbreviated version of the Analysis of the Keyword (LVX) ritual described at the end of chapter 6. After doing so, either move on to whatever practical magick you'd like to perform or simply go about your day.

It might be helpful to research the Rose Cross ritual on the internet and study the writings of other magicians. You never know when you'll come across a diagram or description that will help you understand this practice (and others, for that matter) in a profound way. You could also go old-school and check out Donald Michael Kraig's *Modern Magick* or John Michael Greer's *Monsters: An Investigative Guide to Magical Beings*. These are the two books that were tremendously helpful to me in prison when I had no access to the internet.

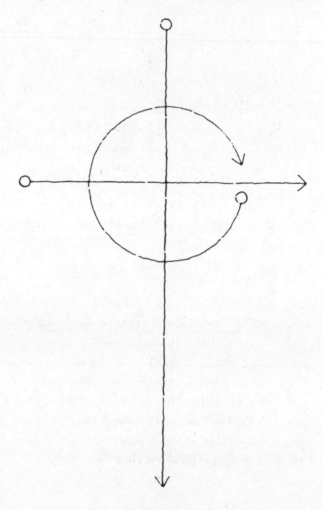

The Rose Cross

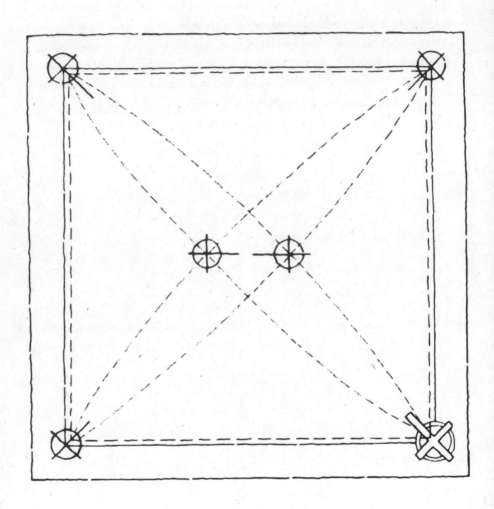

The Rose Cross Ritual Room Diagram

AN INTRODUCTION TO HEXAGRAMS AND THE LESSER BANISHING RITUAL OF THE HEXAGRAM

The hexagrams we use in the following ritual are just geometric patterns consisting of two overlapping triangles resulting in six points. These triangles can overlap in several different ways, including the traditional Star of David pattern, but as the accompanying illustration shows, that's not the only pattern you'll use.

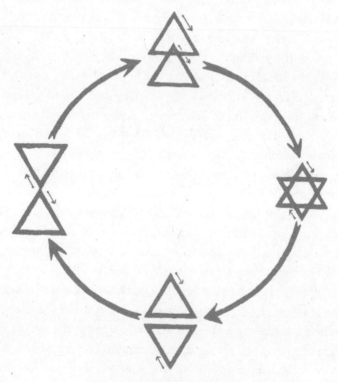

The Lesser Hexagram Ritual

All these triangles should be drawn in golden light and connected together just as you have done elsewhere with a white line. To use the banishing form of the hexagram, draw the figure counterclockwise; to invoke, go clockwise. Draw these symbols directly on top of the blue stars created in the LBRP.

RITUAL: **THE LESSER BANISHING RITUAL OF THE HEXAGRAM**

Mages who strive to purify their intellect, psyche, and aura until only divine energy remains rely heavily on banishing rituals like this one. The Lesser Banishing Ritual of the Hexagram (LBRH) is an incredibly powerful tool for purification, beginning with using it to thoroughly cleanse our environment in order to ensure that there is no energetic residue to pollute us or the magick we perform in our sacred space. That being said, mostly what we're purifying through these banishing rituals is the ego and the levels of our energetic anatomy closest to the material world.

Just as the pentagram corresponds to the elemental aspects of reality, the hexagram is associated with the planetary levels. We also use planetary energies when working with the angels and archangels of the Tree of Life, as well as the angels and archangels of the tarot. Planetary energies are viewed as subtle and rarified, and they belong to a higher plane than elemental energies, which are considered denser and closer to the physical plane. When banishing, the LBRP clears an area of elemental energies and the LBRH purifies a space of planetary energies—the latter is no substitute for the former. You should always do the LBRP before performing practical magick, however, and when performing the LBRH, it should come right after you do the LBRP.

Although hexagrams primarily correlate to planetary energies, they still represent the four elements—it's just that they do so in their celestial form (as in how certain signs of the zodiac are referred to as *air* or *fire* signs, for example). For this reason, when we draw the hexagrams in the four quarters, they don't correspond to the same directions you'll find in the LBRP. For example, in the LBRP, east is associated with air, whereas in the hexagram ritual, east represents fire, because the first sign of the zodiac—Aries—is a fire sign. In this way, the LBRH is based on the triplicity you find in astrology.

1. Perform the LBRP as outlined here in chapter 6 or the one in chapter 13 of *High Magick*.

2. Step forward to the eastern wall of your temple. Directly over the pentagram you drew there for the LBRP, draw a banishing hexagram of fire in golden light. This version of the hexagram is the one that looks like two upward pointing triangles. The hexagrams you'll draw in this ritual appear as if overlaid in front of the pentagrams.

3. Inhale and visualize the earth filling up with light. Place the extended fingers of your sword mudra into the center of the hexagram and see it become brighter as you vibrate the mantra *Ararita* (ar-uh-ree-ta). Technically, *Ararita* isn't a name; it's an acronym for the Hebrew *Achad Rosh Achdotho Rosh Ichudo Temurato Achad*, which means "One is his beginning, one is his individuality, his permutation is one." *Ararita* is a holy word in the sense that it expresses the sentiment that there is only one source from which all things originate, and all things are an expression of that source.

4. Breathe in once more, see the earth infuse with energy, and draw a line of white light from the hexagram you just drew in the east over to the southern wall of your space.

5. Draw the banishing hexagram of earth in golden light in the south just as you did above in step 2, only this time the hexagram looks like the traditional Star of David.

6. Repeat step 3 above, placing your fingers in the hexagram and vibrating the mantra *Ararita*.

7. Take an in-breath, watch as the earth fills up with light, and extend the line of white light from this most recent hexagram over to the western wall of your temple.

8. Inhaling and visualizing the earth's energy as above, draw the banishing hexagram of air here. This is the one that looks like two separated triangles—one facing up, one facing down. Place your extended fingers in the center and see it flare up more brightly as you vibrate the mantra again.

9. Extend the line of white light to the northern wall of your space.

10. In the north, breathe in, watch the earth fill up with energy, and draw the banishing hexagram of water in golden light. This hexagram looks like two triangles facing each other with tips barely touching.

11. Inhale, see the light once more, place your fingers in the middle of the hexagram, and watch it become brighter as you vibrate *Ararita*.

12. Draw the line of white light back over to the original hexagram in the east. Once this is done you should be standing inside a circle of white light with gold, differently shaped hexagrams flaming in all four directions.

13. Standing in the middle of your space, stretch the energy of the circle above your head as if closing a dome above you. Then do the same thing beneath you. At this point, you should be standing in the middle of a sphere of white light.

14. To conclude, perform the abbreviated form of the LVX ritual.

In their invoking form, the LBRP and LBRH together generate an intense amount of elemental and planetary energy that can be channeled to manifest a particular outcome on the material plane or be absorbed into your aura for spiritual sustenance.

RAPID TRANSFORMATION

I think of ceremonial magick as the Western path to enlightenment—the counterpart to many Eastern traditions we're familiar with. Magick is a path, however, that seeks to liberate the individual from the cycle of uncontrolled incarnation in just a single lifetime, as opposed to many, and with the possible exception of Vajrayana Buddhism, this goal makes magick unique among most paths followed today. Accordingly, it's a tradition better suited to those who have psyches more inclined to the stresses of rapid transformation over a more gentle, gradual approach. At its core, magick is about transfiguring the ego into something higher, despite all the techniques to promote manifestation on the material plane. These advanced practices can be used for both, of course, but there's no substitute for using what you find in this chapter for spiritual sustenance.

RITUAL: THE CELESTIAL LOTUS

I call this practice the Celestial Lotus because it best describes the pattern of angelic and archangelic energies that surround me on the astral plane when performing this ritual. I created it after experimenting with a practice called the Supreme Invoking Ritual of the Pentagram and receiving some modifications from my HGA. If you practice magick for long enough, this sort of thing will happen to you as well—you'll suddenly understand a traditional ritual in a fresh way and make adjustments to the practice that make it more meaningful and useful to you, being guided by your HGA along the way. For example, the way I do stage 1 of this ritual entails Metatron, Raziel, and Tzadkiel above me; Sandalphon, Kamael, and Tzaphkiel below me; and Gabriel of Yesod, Michael of Hod, Haniel of Netzach, and Raphael of

Tiphareth around me. After becoming familiar with this version of the practice, feel free to experiment and reorder the angels and archangels as you see fit, because the order of invocation will give the ritual a different feel and will lead to different results.

All of the spheres on the Tree of Life exist within our psyche and aura, and they're usually out of balance in some way due to our current struggles, the nature of our surroundings, or simply because we're energetically depleted. These imbalances play out in the way we think, feel, and behave (even when we're not consciously aware of them), which can lead to depression, addiction, and obsessions of various sorts. The LBRP has the benefit of balancing our elemental energies, but the Celestial Lotus takes the next step and balances our planetary energies as represented on the Tree of Life, as well as correcting the imbalances of zodiacal energies within our aura.

There are three phases, or steps, to the Celestial Lotus ritual. It's incredibly important to go step by step and gradually build up to the final stage, performing the first part at least once a day for at least two weeks before advancing to the second stage. That should be enough time to get a good feel for it and allow you to memorize all of the angels and archangels involved. As in the other practices I've described, the point isn't to rush toward some imaginary finish line but to obtain every ounce of understanding you can at each stage. If you follow the instructions, you'll start to notice a significant change in the way you perceive energy and the astral plane, as well as the way magick feels to you in general. However, you won't be able to exercise the higher aspects of your psyche (the first stage of the awakening process) if you rush into stage 3 without adequate preparation. Just focus on visualizing every aspect of the ritual as thoroughly and richly as possible, and you'll lose yourself in the process and forget all about getting somewhere. The more you can experience the joy of this ritual, the more potent and effective it will be.

I encourage you to be patient with yourself. These advanced rituals are not easy to do, and most people who practice magick never get to this point in the first place. All you really have to do is take your time, do the practices habitually as described, and guard against laziness and the desire to get instant results.

STAGE 1

1. Follow the directions for the LBRP but draw two invoking pentagrams in each quarter instead of just one. Draw the first one (called the *spirit* pentagram) in white light and charge it with the divine name Ararita. Then draw another invoking pentagram (the *elemental* pentagram) in blue light directly on top of the first one, so that the two pentagrams overlap. For the blue pentagrams, you can use the mantras you used in the LBRP—*Yehowah* in the east, *Adonai* in the south, and so on—or charge them with the mantras associated with the planetary energies that correspond with the spheres on the Tree of Life (see end of chapter 2).

2. When you finish this step, you should be standing in the center of a circle of white and blue overlapping pentagrams in each quarter connected with a ring of white light.

3. Now you'll begin to invoke the archangels just as you did in the LBRP, being sure to add Metatron above you and Sandalphon below (the version outlined in *High Magick*). Since this practice is all about the archangels of the Tree of Life, and Metatron and Sandalphon are already represented, you'll be invoking the remaining eight archangels between the four elemental ones you've already called into your sacred space.

4. Between Uriel in the north and Raphael in the east, invoke Michael of Hod.

5. Between Raphael in the east and Michael in the south, invoke Gabriel of Yesod.

6. Between Michael in the south and Gabriel in the west, invoke Haniel of Netzach.

7. Between Gabriel in the west and Uriel in the north, invoke Raphael of Tiphareth.

8. Below you, on either side of Sandalphon, invoke Kamael of Geburah and Tzaphkiel of Binah.

9. Finally, above you on either side of Metatron, invoke Raziel of Chokmah and Tzadkiel of Chesed.

10. As you have done before, visualize pulling the circle of light above you, then below you, such that you are standing in the middle of a sphere of white light. However, this time you are surrounded with the divine energy of fourteen archangels.

11. Conclude with any practical magick you wish to perform or simply end the ritual here, knowing that this tremendous collection of heavenly forces is arranging things on the material plane for your benefit.

When I finish stage 1 of the Celestial Lotus, I have the sensation of almost being able to visibly perceive the archangels surrounding me like a suit of divine armor as I go about my day. It's actually difficult to describe the experience, but it's a tangible sensation that only comes from the intense amount of energy you surround yourself with on the astral plane with this practice. But even that degree of energy pales when compared to the amount you'll generate in the next stage.

STAGE 2

By this point, you should be performing the LBRP, LBRH, and stage 1 of the Celestial Lotus daily. If so, you'll be lit up on the astral level like a spotlight, and you will be sufficiently prepared for stage 2, in which you will add the twelve archangels of the zodiac to the ritual. This means you'll be invoking a total of twenty-six archangels before you reach stage 3. Doing so, you are informing the divine mind and your higher self that you aspire to see through the lens of ultimate reality, in which the individual self is merely an illusion.

1. Immediately after step 9 in stage 1 of this ritual, invoke the twelve zodiacal archangels in a second ring outside of the fourteen archangels you've already called in. Just imagine that the floor is like the face of a giant clock with the numbers 1 through 12 printed on it, and invoke the archangels in a clockwise fashion, beginning with the 12 position. If it helps, you could paint or indicate the numbers on the floor in your space in some other way, but it isn't necessary to do so.

2. As you invoke the archangels in the following order, do your best to visualize them wearing robes of their associated colors. Picture them close together—almost overlapping—such that no external energy could enter your space between them. Invoke them as you did the elemental archangels in the LBRP—inhaling and visualizing them becoming impressively large and magnificent in front of you. As you exhale, vibrate their names (mostly three syllables, but sometimes four) and see them glow brighter with the power of your voice.

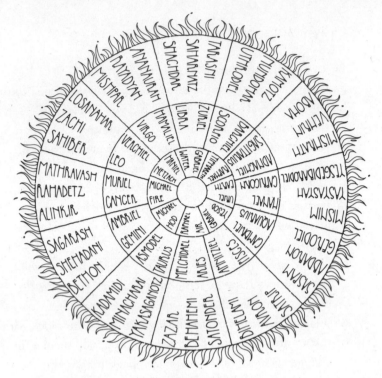

The Celestial Lotus

- 12 Malkhidael, archangel of Aries—red

- 1 Asmodel, archangel of Taurus—red-orange

- 2 Ambriel, archangel of Gemini—orange

- 3 Muriel, archangel of Cancer—amber

- 4 Verchiel, archangel of Leo—gold or yellow

- 5 Hamaliel, archangel of Virgo—yellow-green

- 6 Zuriel, archangel of Libra—emerald green

- 7 Barchiel, archangel of Scorpio—blue-green

- 8 Adnachiel, archangel of Sagittarius—blue

- 9 Hanael, archangel of Capricorn—indigo

- 10 Kambriel, archangel of Aquarius—violet

- 11 Amnitziel, archangel of Pisces—crimson

3. After you've invoked all twelve, stretch your arms out to your sides as if making a cross of your body. As in the LBRP, bring your hands together over your head to close the dome of light above you, and then do the same to close it below you. In the end, you should be standing in the middle of a sphere of divine light.

4. If you're performing this ritual to absorb the gathered energy for spiritual sustenance, you can end here with what's called the License to Depart. Simply say, "I now declare this ritual duly closed. Any spirits trapped herein may now depart, returning to your own abodes and harming none as you do so. Take with you the blessings of Yeheshua." However, if you want to follow these invocations with practical magick, do so before issuing the license, knowing that whatever you direct at this point will carry tremendous power.

With practice and patience, this stage can be done in a half hour or so. If you perform it daily for a year, you'll be astounded by the growth and maturation of your consciousness, because the ritual fosters incredible balance among the various levels and aspects of your energetic anatomy and psyche. Be sure to become thoroughly familiar with stage 2 before moving on to the concluding phase of the ritual; I recommend doing it once a day for several weeks.

STAGE 3

I suggest doing all three stages together every day for at least two weeks, but doing so is quite time consuming and takes a lot of work. It's almost like putting yourself through a Navy Seal–level physical workout every day for two weeks—you can do it, but it probably isn't sustainable for much longer than that. I recommend two weeks to jump-start the process, and then perform the whole Celestial Lotus once a week after that. If you have made it this far in your journey as a magician, you'll still be performing magick in your off days—for example, up through stage 2 (or at least stage 1) of this ritual. Doing so will go fairly quickly by this point.

Stage 3 entails invoking an additional set of zodiacal intelligences you won't find in chapter 3. The angels you'll find here are known as the *decans* of each zodiacal sign. They're basically smaller or less powerful versions of the archangels you invoked in stage 2, and that is how I advise visualizing them. For example, you could imagine that the three decans corresponding to Malkidael (the archangel of Aries) also wear red robes, but that they're all somehow less potent and impressive.

In total, you will be adding thirty-six more angels to those you've already invoked in stages 1 and 2. We break down a circle in 360 degrees, which means that each sign of the zodiac represents 30 degrees of the circle, so each of the decans represents 10 degrees of the circle (three of them for each sign). The point here isn't to give a lesson in basic math but to help you visualize how these angels are situated around your sacred space.

1. After completing step 2 in stage 2 of the Celestial Lotus, you will have invoked twenty-six archangels. This is the point in the ritual to add the angels of the decans, beginning once more with Aries at the 12 position of the visualized clock. The angels of the decans are as follows:

- For Malkidael, archangel of Aries:
  Zazer, Behahemi, Satonder

- For Asmodel, archangel of Taurus:
  Kadamidi, Minacharai, Yakasaganotz

- For Ambriel, archangel of Gemini:
  Sagarash, Shehadani, Bethon

- For Muriel, archangel of Cancer:
  Mathravash, Rahadetz, Alinkir

- For Verchiel, archangel of Leo:
  Losanahar, Zachi, Sahiber

- For Hamaliel, archangel of Virgo:
  Ananaurah, Rayadyah, Mishpar

- For Zuriel, archangel of Libra:
  Tarasni, Saharnatz, Shachdar

- For Barchiel, archangel of Scorpio:
  Kamotz, Nundohar, Uthrodiel

- For Adnachiel, archangel of Sagittarius:
  Mishrath, Vehrin, Aboha

- For Hanael, archangel of Capricorn:
  Misnim, Yasyasyah, Yesgedibarodiel

- For Kambriel, archangel of Aquarius:
  Saspam, Abdaron, Gerodiel

- For Amnitziel, archangel of Pisces:
  Bihelami, Avron, Satrip

2. To begin, picture the archangel Malkidael towering in front of you where you placed him in stage 2. Invoke the first angel of the decans. Inhale and see Zazer expand behind your visualization of Malkidael. Hold your breath for just a moment and then vibrate Zazer's name as you exhale.

3. Now repeat the same process for the next angel, Behahemi, but place him right behind the first, Zazer. Then do the same for the third, Satonder, who goes behind Behahemi.

4. Take a moment to envision the archangel and associated decans all at once.

5. Now continue in a clockwise fashion to the next sign, repeating steps 2 through 4 with the corresponding archangel and angels of the decans as you go.

6. When you complete step 5 above, you'll be surrounded by sixty-two angels and archangels who represent every aspect and nuance of the divine mind as it is manifested in the form of the heavens.

7. Conclude with steps 3 and 4 as outlined in stage 2.

Since there are so many intelligences involved in the Celestial Lotus, feel free to make cheat sheets to peek at as you move repeatedly around the circle of your temple. There's no need to memorize all of them up front or remember who comes in what order, although the more you perform the Celestial Lotus, the easier it all will become.

This is the ritual that led to me first experiencing the dissolution of self. I can't promise the same for anyone else, nor can I fully articulate what the experience was like, but I can say that as a result, I am a lot calmer, more focused, and quite a bit happier. Those are just some of the side effects that come from the incredible amount of spiritual sustenance generated by this practice.

RITUAL: **THE SHEM OPERATION**

There's a Tibetan spiritual tradition called *Dzogchen* ("The Great Perfection") that's most closely identified with Buddhism and the native Bon religion of the Himalayas, but that some experts believe predates both traditions by hundreds if not thousands of years. The advanced practices in Dzogchen result in what's known as the *rainbow body*, in which the adept transmutes their physical form into a nonmaterial body of light upon death and can direct this rainbow body to wherever they wish to travel throughout the cosmos and across the varying levels of reality. There are even documented instances of masters achieving the rainbow body and leaving nothing behind but dust, teeth, or a shrunken version of their former physical body on this side of the divide.

I can't speak on these advanced tantric practices, but I believe that the advanced ceremonial practices in magick result in something like the rainbow body. In fact, I think that the highest practices of most mystical traditions of the world lead to something quite similar, whether it's called the *rainbow body*, the *diamond body* (Taoism), the *solar body* (traditional alchemy), or the *body of light* (the preferred term for ceremonial magicians). Whatever name it goes by, the process of achieving it seems to require some type of purification of the energy system followed by an absorption of higher forms of divine energy through invocation. This is the quickest path to enlightenment—not over the course of millions of lifetimes, but one. And enlightenment is just the beginning. As the Dzogchen masters teach, a being who has completed this many-named process can manifest in any realm—material or spiritual—at will, and intentionally do so in whatever manner it takes to help others cross the abyss.

The practices leading to this profound result are usually a closely guarded secret, mostly due to the fact that it won't work (or, in some instances, might result in insanity or death) for practitioners who haven't completed the preliminaries. In the Western tradition of high magick, this means all of

The Shem Ha Mephorash

the practices leading up to the LBRP, the LBRP as well as relevant modifications to it, and all of the other practices you've encountered in this book up to this point. All of these techniques and rituals must be learned, practiced intensively, and memorized inside and out, so that they are so deeply assimilated into your psyche that they become an integral part of who you are as a conscious and spiritual entity. At that point, you will be prepared to perform the Shem Operation.

It's called that among magicians simply because it's a lot easier than saying "the Invocation of the Seventy-Two Angels of the Shem Ha Mephorash." In ceremonial magick and Qabalah, Shem Ha Mephorash is said to be one of the hidden names of the divine—a name that contains and conveys tremendous power. It's also sometimes called "the explicit name."

I want to stress again that my main goal with this book is to present my own variations on these techniques as clearly as I can, while also pointing you to some resources that are far more capable of giving you a more detailed and nuanced picture. In this case, it's Damon Brand and Chic and Sandra Tabitha Cicero. Anyone interested in the Shem Operation will do themselves a great service by studying the works of these experts. That being said, I strongly recommend that you never confuse information with expertise. My own works and those of others are no substitute for your own practice, discipline, and intent.

The Shem Operation is designed to flood your psyche with a deluge of divine energy, and there's not another practice that empowers you to absorb as much of this energy into your aura for spiritual sustenance. There's really no way to describe the growth it generates in your consciousness and energy field. And when it comes to making things happen on the material plane, the Shem Operation is like harnessing thermonuclear power to manifest your personal desires. For this reason, it is not a practice to be taken lightly. Just as you wouldn't put jet fuel in a single-cylinder lawnmower, you wouldn't perform this ritual in order to manifest anything minor.

The entire Shem Operation isn't something that you'd do every day, although I recommend performing it at least once a week if you can, and only then after mastering all phases of the Celestial Lotus ritual. If you're doing it for spiritual sustenance, I strongly advise performing the Shem Operation at least once a month. There's simply no substitute if you truly want to experience yourself as the mind of God, as opposed to the small, restricted, and individualized ego you typically confuse yourself for.

The Shem Operation is essentially a highly advanced version of the Lesser Invoking Ritual of the Pentagram. For this reason, I won't go into many of the finer details of the practice (for example, the breath work and visualization sequencing), as by this point you will already be more than familiar with them.

The seventy-two angels involved in this ritual correspond with some of the oldest celestial charts of ancient Mesopotamia. You can either invoke all of the different seventy-two angels or choose to focus on one particular angel who corresponds with the practical magick you wish to perform. If the latter suggestion speaks to you, consider your specific need and review the lists in chapter 3 in the section "The Seventy-Two Angels of the Zodiac."

1. Always begin the Shem Operation by performing the LBRP and, if time permits, the LBRH as well. Just the LBRP is okay, but doing both rituals will really clear the way for all of the energies you're about to invoke.

2. As in the Celestial Lotus, draw two pentagrams in each of the four quarters of your space, connecting them with an encircling line of white light. Begin in the east, charging the white spirit pentagram with Ararita and the elemental pentagram with Yahweh.

3. In the south, charge the invoking spirit pentagram with Ararita and the blue pentagram with Adonai.

4. In the west, charge the white pentagram with Ararita and the blue one with Eheieh.

5. Finally, in the north, charge the spirit pentagram with Ararita and the elemental pentagram with Agelah.

6. After connecting these final two pentagrams with the original ones in the east, you should be standing in the center of a circle of white light, with pentagrams in front of you, behind you, and on either side of you.

7. Next, you'll invoke the seventy-two angels of the zodiac (or just one angel seventy-two times) and vibrate each of their names as you do so. There are several ways you can do this. One way is to simply use the clock visualization as before, only this time the clock has seventy-two numbers on it. You could also imagine a pie or pie chart with seventy-two sections. Whatever the case, it's important to create a sphere of angelic energy (including above and below you), regardless of the number or nature of the intelligences you invoke.

8. If performing this ritual in the traditional way, I suggest using a cheat sheet with the names of the seventy-two angels of the zodiac as you walk around your space, as well as any tips to aid in your visualization (their corresponding colors, for example). However, if you're performing the ritual in this manner at least once a week, it won't be long until you memorize most (if not all) of them.

9. After you've envisioned each angel expanding in its place surrounding you and vibrated its name, you should have the psychic sensation of being surrounded by an immense collective of divine force. That's because you are.

10. If you are performing the Shem Operation for spiritual sustenance, simply close the sphere above and below you as before.

11. If invoking these intelligences for practical magick, direct the energy into a chosen object or visualization. For example, if you want to place the energy into a candle, position it in the middle of your space, inhale, see all of the pentagrams and angels grow as bright and vivid as you possibly can, hold this breath and image for about four seconds, exhale, and then watch as everything you've visualized transforms into a blast of light that travels directly into the candle. See all of that energy collapse into the candle and saturate it with divine power. Actually, a candle is a particular receptacle for energy, because most people choose to let it burn down and then place the remaining wax in a location of their choosing. You can also direct the energy into a sigil or talisman (as described in chapter 7) as a receptacle for the collected energy, or put it into a visualization. For example, if I were doing this ritual for better health for myself, I'd visualize an image of me above my altar and try to picture myself doing something symbolic of that desire—in this case, me smiling and feeling happy because I'm completely healthy. Then I inhale, hold the breath and image of all the pentagrams and angels, exhale, and watch everything I've envisioned collapse into that picture of myself, saturating it with so much divine light that the details of the visualization disappear—I just know there's an image of me in there somewhere.

12. Regardless of my primary reasons for performing the Shem Operation, I always conclude by closing the sphere above and below me and issuing a license to depart (some version of the one in stage 2 of the Celestial Lotus).

Although the traditional way of performing this ritual involves seventy-two angels, you could invoke more if you so choose. I have, at times, employed hundreds of images of the same angel. Further elaboration is not necessary, but I suggest trying it out when you have the time. Every time you invoke a given angel, you pull a little bit more of its energy into your space. It should be noted here that as an expression of the divine mind, each angel entails an infinite amount of energy.

No matter how you choose to do the Shem Operation, in the end you will have invoked an incredible amount of energy into your aura, and that will bring about a tremendous unfolding in your consciousness when done with regularity. I experienced two profound results through this ritual. First, I discovered more peace in my life than ever before and felt a significant decrease in clinging and attachment to particular desires. As the Buddha taught, since suffering is caused by attachment, when clinging fades, so too does our suffering.

Second, I inexplicably began to download information after performing the Shem Operation for some time, and this new information has been the beginning of the next phase in my life as an artist, magician, and teacher. I actually think of it as my own personal quest for the Holy Grail, which I'll say a little bit more about now in "Next Steps."

NEXT STEPS

Magick is a highly individualized path. No two magicians will follow the same trajectory, connect with the same divine intelligences, visualize details of rituals in the same way, or be influenced by the same teachers and expert sources. That being said, there are two particular goals that are essential in high magick, and anyone who truly wishes to progress in this tradition should consider them both with a lot of curiosity and sincerity. The first goal is crossing the abyss. The second is what's traditionally called *achieving the knowledge and conversation of the Holy Guardian Angel.* I spoke at some length about crossing the abyss in the introduction, so now—in the conclusion of this book—I'd like to leave you with some thoughts about connecting with the Holy Guardian Angel (most often referred to as the HGA).

There's quite a bit of confusion about what we mean by the HGA in magick. Even though the HGA is typically identified as one's higher self (especially in New Age circles), it's usually experienced as a separate being that is completely independent of the practitioner. When we first begin to catch glimpses of the HGA in our practice and daily life, it feels as if we are receiving guidance from some powerful external entity, and so we speak of the HGA as if it were such a being. Part of this is simply shorthand; part of it is because this is our actual experience until we are more fully integrated with this aspect of ourselves.

Historically, ceremonial magicians believed that the human soul consisted of four parts and that most people only operate through the two lower aspects—the *nephesh* and the *ruach*. In Freudian terms, the nephesh most closely correlates to the id and is considered to be the lowest, most primal part of our soul. It's the source of all our instincts, appetites, and desires—the level we share with other members of the animal kingdom. The ruach would be more like Freud's ego—the thinking, scheming, intellectual part of the soul. This aspect of ourselves is typically so active in most people that we regularly confuse ourselves for it, thinking that the ego is all we are.

The HGA is the third part of the soul—the *neshamah*. We don't normally experience this part of ourselves except through spiritual practices such as meditation and ritual. But when we do get to know the HGA, we realize that there's a lot more going on than the limited egoic part of us. With practice and diligence, we can align the HGA with the ruach and nephesh such that the three function harmoniously together. In magick, this union is sometimes represented with the symbology of marriage—we are said to be "wed" to our HGA. Attaining the knowledge and conversation of the HGA is the next step in humanity's evolutionary journey, and I believe that at their best, all religions are designed to help facilitate this process in some way.

The highest part of the soul is called the *chiah*. Once activated, it allows us to directly experience ourselves as the divine—as indistinguishable from the source itself—and not in a mere, factual way. Through the chiah, we finally understand that the individual self is an illusion, that only the divine exists, and that this consciousness transcends time and space. This understanding allows us to relinquish all attachments to the material plane and our physical form.

Connecting with the HGA is an incredibly important milestone in the practice of magick. It allows you to become familiar with your true will—the reason you manifested in this particular life in this particular place, as well as the best path of action to help you act in harmony with the entire universe. Achieving knowledge and conversation with the HGA also means that you are developing the rainbow body (as discussed in the Shem Operation)—the body of light that enables you to carry your consciousness and senses beyond the confines of your physical body. Through purification rituals and invocations, this body of light gradually becomes more prominent, gaining in power and abilities as we progress through ever higher levels of spiritual development.

THE INFECTION

It feels like my senses have been scoured clean. Like for the first time in my life I can actually see, hear, and even think clearly. And I can finally notice the extent to which fear has been the main motivating force of my actions up to this point. I have been afraid since the day I was born, and I have clung to that fear so tightly, with everything I had. I'm still afraid, but there's something fundamentally different about it. It rises and falls away, and it's no longer difficult to let it go. I don't cling to fear anymore, and therefore I don't feed it. I can also see now just how much fear runs the lives of people I meet or see all around me, not to mention the world as a whole. People fear aging, sickness, financial hardship, discomfort, embarrassment, lack of meaning, isolation, dying . . . you name it. They fear for themselves, for the people they love, for the environment, for everything. They fear their enemies and detractors, they fear chaos, they fear the unknown. They fear that there is no God, they fear that there is a God—that they will somehow be found lacking. To make matters worse, this fear is contagious. The ego spreads it from person to person like a virus—mouth to ear, heart to heart. The worst part of it all is that most people don't even see it—their fear runs their lives into the dirt like a malevolent machine. That's why I spend so much time trying to encourage people to stop worrying, to turn their focus instead on the light. If all of humanity is a form of organism, those of us committed to waking up must act like white blood cells in order to counteract the infection of fear.

The ancient book *The Book of Abramelin* describes a system of magick developed by an Egyptian magician especially devoted to discovering one's HGA. The rituals entailed in the process are complex and arduous, requiring near-constant practice and devotion for at least eighteen months (although one translator cut the process down to six months), and also asserting that the magician must abstain from certain enjoyments (namely, sex and alcohol) during that time. There's also a section in the book that describes how to make a particular kind of oil, known among magicians as Abramelin oil, found in Exodus 30:1—"And thou shalt make an altar to burn incense upon: of shittim wood shalt thou make it" (KJV). I've tried to make the oil myself and discovered right away that some of the ingredients seem to directly oppose others—for example, myrrh restricts, binds, and banishes, whereas frankincense promotes expansion, growth, and development. At first I found this to be confusing—this particular combination, for example, felt like trying to banish and invoke or inhale and exhale at the same time. But the more I paid attention to the process, I began to see that all of the ingredients in the oil were meant to represent all of the energies on the Tree of Life. Applying the oil would be like anointing someone with the entire spectrum of divine energies.

Fortunately, you don't need to purchase a translation of *The Book of Abramelin* or go through the arduous process of making esoteric oils in order to contact your HGA. Another way to do so that's found across various religions is through the path of devotion—intense adoration of Christ or the Virgin Mary in Catholicism, forms of deity yoga in Tibetan Buddhism, or bhakti as it's found in Hinduism. Aleister Crowley even created a devotional ritual for ceremonial magicians he called the *Liber Astarte*, in which an individual devotes their practice to invoking a deity of love and meditating on that deity until they work themselves into a frenzy of longing.

Yet another way to connect to your HGA is to commit yourself to the practices outlined in this book, the crux of which is the Shem Operation. In my opinion, doing so accomplishes everything described in the Abramelin ritual, and with enough dedication, the Shem Operation will invariably help you establish contact with the HGA. That's just one of the primary goals of high magick, of course, but achieving it will play out in amazing ways you never could have predicted.

When I began all of these practices in earnest, I could wrap my mind around connecting with my HGA, but the idea of crossing the abyss just seemed fantastical to me. I knew that magick had saved my life, protected me in prison, assisted in my release, and worked for all sorts of other practical reasons, but *enlightenment* seemed something that ancient masters did in caves on the other side of the world. I wasn't even sure it could be done anymore, especially by me. I was invoking all of these archangels and angels because it felt good—I liked feeling cleansed, clarified, and empowered by the rituals and influx of divine energy. For me, that was good enough. But inadvertently (but probably not) something else—something greater—began to happen.

It all started with me invoking the four archangels of the elements and then adding Sandalphon and Metatron to the LBRP. That worked so well that I added the archangels of the Tree of Life. After getting used to that extra amount of energy and memorizing all of the names and corresponding colors and so on, I started adding the twelve archangels of the zodiac. After working with this combined collection of intelligences for several weeks, I realized that I was no longer experiencing any symptoms of PTSD. I also felt unusually blissful, and my mind was focused on thoughts of the divine almost constantly. All of this encouraged me to devote myself even more to magick.

I knew at the core of my being that something big was coming, that I was doing exactly what I was supposed to be doing, and this deep knowing made me press ahead. That's when I began to add the seventy-two zodiacal angels cataloged in chapter 3. At first I only did this once a day, mostly because it was taking me about three hours to complete the ritual. But then the results were so astounding that I worked up to twice a day, then three times. I started going to bed at ten at night and waking up at two or so in the morning just so I could get more magick in during the day. In a way, it was exhausting, but I also felt energized and excited. All of the visualizations were becoming brighter and more vibrant in a way I'd never experienced before. I knew that what I was doing was incredibly powerful and right, and that encouraged me to push forward even more.

Then one morning when I was in the middle of the angelic invocations involved in the Shem Operation, I experienced something that was initially disorienting and frightening. Suddenly it felt like the very earth dropped away beneath my feet. I was surrounded by an incredible amount of light—it was so bright that it felt like I was standing in the middle of the sun. Then it felt like something snapped, and I was surrounded by the darkness of an infinite void. My first thought was that I'd broken something—like, maybe I'd burned out a meridian with too much chi or something. Even though I didn't know it at the time, I was experiencing the complete and absolute destruction of the self. That part of me I had for so long believed was all of *me* disintegrated before my eyes like a handful of dust tossed into the wind. It was truly like being lost in a storm, and it was terrifying.

The accompanying sensations of that experience lasted for about three days. I thought I was slowly dying and that soon I'd cease to exist. But on the third day I realized that there was a part of me that was watching all of this happen—that even as what I knew as *I* was clearly falling away, there was another *I*—some form of consciousness that was observing the disintegration. That realization was like a switch flipping, because after that I felt absolute calm—all of my previous fear just vanished. And that's when I saw it.

The closest I'll ever be able to come to articulating what happened is this: I saw the nighttime sky. It was crystal clear—truly beautiful. And then, across this vision of the sky, I saw a word spelled out, just as if the wind were gently rippling across the stars as if they were wheat. The word was *Enlil.*

I'd never seen or heard it before in my life. I had no idea what it meant, but it was simultaneously beautiful and puzzling, and it continued to appear in my mind repeatedly over the next few days. I was so awestruck by the whole experience that it took me a couple of days to remember that I could search for the word on the internet. Within minutes I discovered that Enlil is an ancient name to describe divinity that dates all the way back to the very origin of known human societies—ancient Mesopotamia. Enlil was in fact the chief deity of their pantheon, and the Sumerians described his presence as so brilliant that not even the other gods could look upon him.

HISTORY OF MAGICK: IN THE BEGINNING

The Sumerian creation story asserts that divine intelligences created humankind so that we could take up their work. Some people say that this means aliens from another planet created us to be slaves here on earth, but what the Sumerian tablets actually say sounds a lot like what we read in the book of Genesis 1:26—"Let us make man in our image, after our likeness: and let them have dominion . . . over all the earth" (KJV). According to the Sumerians, after we were created in their likeness, the gods withdrew and intended for us to pick up where they left off. We were meant to forge ahead and improve upon what they had started by shaping reality and creating heaven here on earth. In other words, we were meant to be something potent and holy—the exact opposite of slaves. Some of our holy books (the Bible, the Quran, and the Torah, to name a few) allude to this, but mostly they describe the lives and stories of people who practiced magick of one form or another. These tomes do not necessarily reveal the techniques they used—that's something passed down from master to apprentice throughout time. You may have heard this referred to as the oral tradition, which points to more than stories—it actually indicates the practice of the magician using their voice to transmit a current of energy that ties the student to a lineage of teachings that go all the way back to ancient Mesopotamia. This is the true meaning of the scripture found in John 1:1, "In the beginning was the Word, and the Word was with God, and the Word was God" (KJV).

So, of course, I began invoking him. Instead of calling upon all of the angelic intelligences I'd been using, I invoked Enlil in all directions—east, west, up, down, and everywhere in between. The resultant energy I experienced was unlike anything I'd ever felt, even after years of intense angel work. Enlil's presence was like feeling the unified power of a thousand archangels. If invoking an archangel were akin to the force of a stick of dynamite going off, invoking Enlil would be more like the explosion of a hydrogen bomb. I didn't thoroughly understand who or what Enlil was at the time, but the experience of being with him was so profound that I became consumed with devotion and adoration. There was no me; there was only love for the divine. It felt as if all of the borders I'd known had simply dissolved and there was nothing left but Enlil. And it is through invoking him and practicing in this way that I began to download an entirely new type of information. I began to understand the history of magick as never before, and I began to detect particular currents of energy at work through the evolution of human civilization. A sense of peace and power started to grow in me with every passing day, as it continues to do so now, over a year later.

As Beethoven wrote to his patron, the Archduke Rudolph, "There is no loftier mission than to approach the Divinity nearer than other men, and to disseminate the divine rays among mankind."[1] After we become liberated from the illusion of self, we are charged with assisting others with our particular gifts, just as the bodhisattvas in Buddhism pledge to do until every single being is liberated. In magick, we first initiate this process by calling in more and more

divinity through our purified physical form, which eventually leads to contacting our HGA and crossing the abyss. When that happens, it's said that magicians return from the experience with a *magickal child*—a gift of great importance. For me, that gift is my developing connection to Enlil.

THE PATH OF THE BODHISATTVA

I had a recent vision of my master in Japan, Harada Roshi—the one who sat with me on death row when I was waiting to die. In the vision I saw Roshi in his true form—a bodhisattva who could have chosen a different path after he crossed the abyss but who instead decided to wait on this side of eternal bliss and hold the door open for the rest of us. It makes me weep to feel that rare level of love and beauty, and when I contact it, I can see it everywhere I look. That's who I want to be too—completely absorbed in my higher self and empowered to help others in any way that I can. I lived alone in a burning nest of fear, rage, and horror for so long, and now that I'm on the other side, it's my task to see that I'm not alone anymore and that others need my help. A big part of my path now is learning to love the world, to actually enjoy life, and to help steward the divine garden that's been given to us. That's exactly what Harada Roshi has done—not because he had to but rather he can't imagine not doing so. My whole heart is in it now—there's just too much I love, and so many people. So, I'll stay until the very end and help clean up after the party.

I want to share some of this new work with you before closing, but in truth it will take an entirely new book to even get at half of it. It's simply too profound and compelling. That being said, I'll do my best to summarize some of it here and hope you'll be interested enough to follow up later.

When we invoke angels and archangels, what we're essentially doing is invoking the very energy of stars and groupings of stars. The ancient Sumerians divided the celestial sphere into three parts—northern, southern, and central—and knew each part as an infinitely powerful divine intelligence. They called the being identified with the Southern Hemisphere Enki, and the central region (basically, the stars populating the sky above the equator) was known as Anu. Enlil was the deity associated with the Northern Hemisphere. Together, these three—Enki, Anu, and Enlil—composed one of the first holy trinities on record. This explains why invoking Enlil was so unbelievably powerful to me—I was essentially calling up an entire third of the celestial sphere. The energy I was gathering from all of the angels and archangels I'd been invoking before paled in comparison.

One of the things I downloaded by invoking Enlil regards the lamassu that I mentioned in the introduction to part 1 of this book. They're ancient beings depicted in sculptures and carvings all throughout the Middle East (as well as on the cover of this book)—amalgamations of four different creatures: a lion, a bull, an eagle, and a human. They are, in fact, the first representations of archangels we know of in human history. At some point in time, the four creatures that make up the lamassu were initially depicted as winged people, became incorporated into Christianity, and would come to represent the Gospels of Matthew, Mark, Luke, and John. Before that, however, the lamassu were visual cyphers for essential information to the people of that time—namely, that the four creatures represent four signs of the zodiac: the lion for Leo, the bull for Taurus, the eagle for Scorpio, and the human for Aquarius.

In this carving of Christ you can see four creatures: a lion, a bull, an eagle, and a man. They represent the four fixed signs of the zodiac: Leo, Taurus, Scorpio, and Aquarius. In the aura around Christ, the twelve archangels of the zodiac are being invoked into his energy field. Such works of art were not created just to be aesthetically pleasing. They were meant to convey instructions, to make sure the information could still be found even if language was forgotten forever. We have forgotten where we came from and don't know where we're supposed to be going. Magick is the way to remember. Carving by Andrea da Giona, 1434 CE. Photo by Damien Echols, The Cloisters, New York, New York.

Please keep in mind that I only received a ninth-grade education (and probably not a great one, at that), and I am certainly no expert when it comes to astronomy, but from what I can figure, somewhere around 10500 BCE, the sun would have risen in Leo at the spring equinox. If you were watching the sun rise at that time in the east, the constellation of Aquarius would be at your back, Scorpio would be on your right, and Taurus would be on your left. Although there's plenty of debate on the subject, the Orion correlation theory asserts that this is about the same time when the Great Sphinx of Giza was constructed, and it would have also been facing the constellation of Leo at the spring equinox (hence, it has the body of a lion).

Somewhere in the middle of the devotional experience I described before, I started spending a lot of time at the Metropolitan Museum of Art in New York. They had an exhibit from ancient Mesopotamia, and I'd just sit there for hours to soak in as much energy as I could from the depictions of the lamassu and other artifacts. In Sumer, statues weren't just used to represent a deity—they actually were constructed in order to house that energy. The deity's energy was invoked repeatedly and directed into the object, much in the same way as we use magick to charge talismans and amulets, except infinitely more powerful. The Sumerians basically created earthly containers for the divine intelligence to reside on the material plane, and the temples that housed these statues and carvings were considered to be the houses of that particular god. It wasn't a metaphor to them—it was real. And all of the energy placed into these holy objects doesn't just vanish because they're in a museum on Fifth Avenue (or wherever they happen to be) instead of some temple thousands of years ago in the Fertile Crescent. The power is still there, and when you spend time with blessed artifacts like those, you can bathe in their energy for all sorts of beneficial effects on your consciousness and energetic body.

When I wasn't at the museum, I was at home invoking Enlil in various rituals, sometimes up to a hundred times in all directions. I'd finish one of these practices and there wouldn't be a single thought in my head. I just experienced a state of alert presence with no concept of past or future, just standing there by myself in the middle of my temple, eyes closed, whispering or humming. On one occasion I was straining so hard in the practice that I was unaware of how hard I'd been grinding my teeth until I felt the grit of a broken filling on my tongue.

In the middle of one of these intense sessions, I was told to open my eyes. I say *told*, but I didn't actually hear a voice saying it. Neither was it something I merely felt. I actually don't know how to articulate precisely how I perceived the command, I just know that when I received it, I recognized it as a divine directive of some sort. So I did what the nonvoice voice told me to do: I opened my eyes.

Immediately in front of me was a talismanic painting I'd made about a year before. It's just a simple black cypher on a white background that's unintelligible to anyone who doesn't know the code. All it says is "May the light protect, guide, and illuminate me," over and over again. Anyway, when I opened my eyes on it this time, most of the painting appeared blurry, almost as if I couldn't focus on the individual symbols. The only thing that popped out to me was something right in the middle of the canvas. It said "Lil."

I still have that painting hanging up in my room. No matter how many times I've looked at it, scanning every line for the word *Lil* to reappear, it never has. But I found out what it means in Sumerian—it's the word for "heaven" (or "the heavens"). I also understand that it's my *word*—the embodiment of everything I have to teach. Moses's word was *YHVH*, Lao Tzu's was *Tao*, and mine is *Lil*. My paradigm for helping people replicate my results is found in Lil—in the heavens, in the stars.

HISTORY OF MAGICK: THE CURRENT OF ENLIL

High magick is a current of energy that extends all the way back to ancient Mesopotamia. For thousands of years, the city of Nippur was considered a sacred site where rulers from around the known world would travel to undergo initiation and receive empowerment at Ekur, the temple of Enlil.

If a ruler left the temple without bearing the current of Enlil's energy, they were not seen as a legitimate king. This initiation process was created to assist kings in ruling their lands benevolently and to help them shape the evolution of humanity, and the more current the king carried, the more prosperous his lands would become. Needless to say, whenever the king brought the current back to his kingdom, it underwent cultural modifications of all sorts, until what was once called Enlil became known by thousands of other names throughout the world. The Hebrews received this current as the tetragrammaton YHVH—a name regarded as too sacred to be uttered. Over time, those initiated into the current became more territorial about it, seeking greater control over its usage. Anyone found to be practicing magick without approval would regularly be executed, although the current itself is far less discriminating. Since the time of Enlil, the current was designed to be passed on, and it always finds ways to circumvent human restrictions and structures, especially if its recipient has been made receptive by the practice of magick. That being said, as the current spread throughout the Middle East and Europe (by way of the Knights Templar), its outward forms became increasingly diluted, much like in the game known as Chinese whispers or telephone, in which the first person whispers something into a person's ear, and that person whispers what they heard into another person's ear, and so on and so on. And so it was with magick. The mangled result of centuries of dilution is the magickal system presented by the Hermetic Order of the Golden Dawn.

If I can accurately describe the new information I'm downloading, as well as what I have experienced and the steps I took to trigger those experiences, then perhaps others with a consciousness similar to mine will be able to duplicate the process, or at least experience some version of it in their own way, and all of this is the ever-expanding subject of my forthcoming book.

NOTES

INTRODUCTION

1. "About A∴A∴," Astrum Argentum, astrumargenteum.org /en/about-us.

CHAPTER 1: ARCHANGELS OF THE ELEMENTS

1. Gregg Braden, *Secrets of the Lost Mode of Prayer: The Hidden Power of Beauty, Blessing, Wisdom, and Hurt* (Carlsbad, CA: Hay House, 2016).

PART 2: PRACTICES AND RITUALS

1. "What Is the Super Radiance Effect?" World Peace Group, worldpeacegroup.org/super_radiance.html.

CHAPTER 5: MIND TRAINING, MINDFULNESS, AND MEDITATION

1. John Michael Greer, "Foundations of Magical Practice: Meditation," Ecosophia: Toward an Ecological Spirituality, ecosophia.net /blogs-and-essays/the-well-of-galabes /foundations-of-magical-practice-meditation.

CHAPTER 7: CALLING ON ANGELS

1. Rick Hanson, "Take in the Good," rickhanson.net/ take-in-the-good.

NEXT STEPS

1. Ludwig van Beethoven, *Beethoven: The Man and the Artist, As Revealed in His Own Words*, ed. Friedrich Kerst, trans. Henry Krehbiel (New York: Huebsch, 1905).

RESOURCES

I want to take this opportunity to provide you with a few other leads to follow for further learning and development. These works have helped me tremendously in my own practice as well as in the research I put into this book. I highly recommend delving into as many of these authors and books as possible:

Brand, Damon. *Archangels of Magick: Rituals for Prosperity, Healing, Love, Wisdom, Divination, and Success*. Self-published, Amazon Digital Services, 2018.

————. *The 72 Angels of Magick: Instant Access to the Angels of Power*. Self-published, CreateSpace, 2016.

Cicero, Chic, and Sandra Tabitha Cicero. *Tarot Talismans: Invoke the Angels of the Tarot*. Woodbury, MN: Llewellyn Publishers, 2006.

Davidson, Gustav. *A Dictionary of Angels: Including the Fallen Angels*. New York: Free Press, 1994.

Greer, John Michael, *Monsters: An Investigator's Guide to Magical Beings*. Woodbury, MN: Llewellyn Publishers, 2001.

Greer, John Michael, Clare Vaughn, and Earl King, Jr. *Learning Ritual Magic: Fundamental Theory and Practice for the Solitary Apprentice*. Newburyport, MA: Weiser Books, 2004.

Kraig, Donald Michael. *Modern Magick: Twelve Lessons in the High Magickal Arts*. Woodbury, MN: Llewellyn Publishers, 2010.

Louv, Jason. *John Dee and the Empire of Angels: Enochian Magick and the Occult Roots of the Modern World*. Rochester, VT: Inner Traditions, 2018.

RavenWolf, Silver. *Angels: Companions in Magick*. Woodbury, MN: Llewellyn Publishers, 2002.

Woodcroft, Ben. *Angelic Sigils, Keys, and Calls: 142 Ways to Make Instant Contact with Angels and Archangels*. Self-published, 2017.

I also strongly recommend checking out the Gallery of Magick collective (galleryofmagick.com) and the work of Gregg Braden, host of the Gaia series *Missing Links*.

INDEX

Page numbers in italics refer to images.

ABOUT THE AUTHOR

Damien Echols is a ceremonial magician who spent eighteen years on death row in Arkansas for a crime he did not commit. Damien and the two other men convicted of the crime became known as the West Memphis Three, and they were the subject of a three-part documentary series by HBO called *Paradise Lost*, as well as *West of Memphis*, a documentary produced by Peter Jackson. All three men were finally released in 2011.

While on death row, Damien received ordination into the Rinzai Zen tradition. His *New York Times* bestselling book *Life After Death* was published after his release, as well as *Yours for Eternity*. His third book, *High Magick: A Guide to the Spiritual Practices that Saved My Life on Death Row*, was published in 2018 by Sounds True.

Damien currently lectures on ceremonial magick and teaches classes around the world while also working as a visual artist. His artwork entails ritually devised glyphs, sigils, and symbols designed to bypass the egoic consciousness and interact directly with the higher self. It combines magick techniques with his own alphabet and writing system to break down concepts and scenarios into abstract designs.

Damien and his wife, Lorri Davis, live with their three cats in Harlem in New York City.

For more information, visit damienechols.com or find him on Facebook, Instagram @damienechols, or Twitter @Damienechols.

ABOUT SOUNDS TRUE

Sounds True is a multimedia publisher whose mission is to inspire and support personal transformation and spiritual awakening. Founded in 1985 and located in Boulder, Colorado, we work with many of the leading spiritual teachers, thinkers, healers, and visionary artists of our time. We strive with every title to preserve the essential "living wisdom" of the author or artist. It is our goal to create products that not only provide information to a reader or listener but also embody the quality of a wisdom transmission.

For those seeking genuine transformation, Sounds True is your trusted partner. At SoundsTrue.com you will find a wealth of free resources to support your journey, including exclusive weekly audio interviews, free downloads, interactive learning tools, and other special savings on all our titles.

To learn more, please visit SoundsTrue.com/freegifts or call us toll-free at 800.333.9185.